The Walter Lynwood Fleming
Lectures in Southern History

Louisiana State University

The Creation of Confederate Nationalism

The Creation of
Confederate Nationalism

Ideology and Identity
in the Civil War South

Drew Gilpin Faust

Louisiana State University Press
Baton Rouge

Designer: Diane B. Didier
Typeface: Trump Mediaeval
Typesetter: The Composing Room of Michigan, Inc.

Library of Congress Cataloging-in-Publication Data

Faust, Drew Gilpin.
The creation of Confederate nationalism : ideology and identity in
the Civil War South / Drew Gilpin Faust.
  p.   cm. — (The Walter Lynwood Fleming lectures in southern
history)
  Bibliography: p.
  Includes index.

      1. Nationalism—Confederate States of America.   2. Confederate
States of America—History.   I. Title.   II. Series.
E487.F38 1988
973.7'42—dc 19   88-9036
                                                        CIP
ISBN 0-8071-1606-8 (paperbound)

The paper in this book meets the guidelines for permanence and durability
of the Committee on Production Guidelines for Book Longevity of the
Council on Library Resources. ∞

Louisiana Paperback Edition, 1989
   07 06   10 9 8

For Jessica

Contents

Preface and Acknowledgments   xiii

I   The Problem of Confederate Nationalism   1

II   "A Nation to Do His Work upon Earth": Religion,
      Politics, and Confederate Nationalism   22

III   "Sliding into the World": The Sin of Extortion and the
      Dynamic of Confederate Identity   41

IV   "God Will Not Be Mocked": Confederate Nationalism
      and Slavery Reform   58

V   Conclusion   82

      Notes   87
      Index   107

Illustrations

Hair sculpture by J. Emma Conrad   9

Sheet music, "The Southern Marseillaise"   12

Sheet music, "The Beauregard Manassas Quick-Step"   20

The Great Seal of the Confederacy   25

Cartoon, *Southern Women Feeling the Effects of Rebellion and Creating Bread Riots*   53

Playbill for a performance of the Confederate Nightingales   66

Sheet music, "I'm Coming to My Dixie Home"   68

Painting, *The Burial of Latané* by William D. Washington   69

Preface and Acknowledgments

The essays that follow are a revised and somewhat expanded version of the Walter Lynwood Fleming Lectures that I delivered in April, 1987, at Louisiana State University. I am grateful for both the honor and the opportunity that the occasion offered. I found that the lecture genre encouraged both speculation and synthesis, challenging me to confront old problems in new ways. It is my hope that the result of my effort will challenge its readers as well.

I am deeply indebted to a number of individuals and institutions for assistance in this undertaking. The University of Pennsylvania has supported my scholarship with extraordinary generosity, ranging from the library's willing purchase of microfilm to the very tangible sorts of encouragement I have received from administrators Michael Aiken, Walter Wales, Thomas Ehrlich, and Sheldon Hackney. I cannot imagine any university doing more. I am also most grateful to the John Simon Guggenheim Memorial Foundation and the American Council of Learned Societies for fellowship aid. Librarians at every collection cited have been unfailingly helpful. I would like to offer special thanks to Cynthia English of the Boston Athenaeum, Ellen Gartrell of the William R. Perkins Library, Duke University, and Nelson Lankford of the Virginia Historical Society.

I have imposed shamelessly on my fellow scholars for assistance and advice throughout my work on this project. Richard Beringer, Eugene Genovese, Steven Hahn, Peter Kolchin, Elizabeth Long, Stephanie McCurry, Reid Mitchell, and Janice Radway read and criticized the entire manuscript. They have saved me from several important errors and have suggested changes that I have incorporated into the book. I hope they know how much their generosity has meant to me as well as to this work. I hope, too, they will forgive me for sometimes ignoring their advice. In ways ranging from the mundane to the transcendent, Charles Rosenberg has made this book intellectually and personally possible.

The Creation of Confederate Nationalism

I

The Problem of Confederate Nationalism

In the years since Confederates stacked their rifles at Appomattox, Americans North and South have struggled to understand the conflict that cost more than 600,000 lives and nearly destroyed the nation itself. The causes of the war have provided one major focus of controversy, but perhaps even more intellectual and moral energy has been devoted to determining how and why the North was victorious. The debate has been anything but dispassionate, for many of the participants have seemed—even in the mid-twentieth century—to share the belief of their nineteenth-century forebears that the war's outcome represented a divine judgment. Southerners (and southern historians) have tended to view the question less as one of explaining northern victory than exploring southern loss, the failure that imposed on future generations the "burden of southern history." Confederate defeat became for many southerners an expression of the region's moral inadequacies. As historian E. Merton Coulter stated bluntly in 1950, the South lost because it did "not deserve to win."[1]

Yet a widely shared sense of failure did not imply consensus about the precise nature of the South's shortcomings, and these disagreements have persisted to the present day. The first generation of postwar southerners found it easiest to stress the objective, tangible reasons for southern defeat: northern preponderancy in men and materiel, and the inevitable disadvantages of an agricultural civilization confronted with a modern technological war.

Late nineteenth-century propagandists of the New South Creed and adherents of the Myth of the Lost Cause could agree that the South had failed through sins of omission rather than commission, through inadvertence rather than active wrongdoing, through the failure to industrialize during the antebellum period rather than as a result of adherence to flawed military, political, or social principles.[2]

Some modern scholars have focused on similar factors in their explanations of southern defeat, arguing that because the South was inferior from the outset in every objective necessity for waging war, the Confederacy simply did not have a chance. But such arguments, at least in their purest form of a simple totting up of available resources, have been few, partly because of the weaknesses inherent in any such one-dimensionality, and partly, as well, one suspects, because of their failure to address those more abstract issues of moral right that have resided at the heart of the controversy. Even today, we are still debating whether Appomattox was the South's punishment for the sin of slavery.[3]

Almost all explanations of Confederate defeat have thus dealt in some way with southern ideology, with the South's subjective image of itself and its war goals, with the peculiarities of this vision in contrast with that of the North, and with the way this belief system shaped mobilization of the resources the Confederacy did have available for its pursuit of victory. Variously cast as discussions of Confederate morale, esprit de corps, identity, or will to fight, such considerations are all, in their most general form, part of the extensive historiographical exploration of southern nationalism, of how Confederates defined themselves and their commitment to a common, corporate existence. In the context of secession and war, nationalism became synonymous with the effort by leaders of this struggle for independence to articulate an ideology appropriate to their ends.[4]

The problem of southern nationalism, whether myth or reality, has become, in the words of historian Steven Channing, a "venerable historical chestnut." Yet we seem little further along toward understanding its sources, meaning, and impact than we were in 1963, when David Potter published an essay that remains the most cogent statement of the perils and possibilities in the undertaking. "What appears on its face to be a mere observational or descriptive statement about psychological attitudes may be in fact an indirect form of argumentation about the validity of a set of political claims," Potter cautioned. Despite his warnings, historians have continued to fall into the trap of using nationalism as a valuative rather than descriptive concept, as a kind of mask for those moral judgments that, even a century after the fact, seem inseparable from any consideration of the Civil War. Scholars have continued to fear that accepting the reality of Confederate nationalism would somehow imply its legitimacy, or in Potter's words, "validate the right of a proslavery movement to autonomy and self-determination."[5]

Since Potter's premature death in 1971, the questions of nationalism and of the intangible components of military success have become further embroiled in presentist concerns as a result of late-twentieth-century America's own experience in Vietnam. It is difficult to argue that the South's industrial unpreparedness for modern war made southern defeat inevitable when the example of North Vietnam snatching victory from the American superpower is still so immediate in our minds. If North Vietnam could win, why not the South? Why did Appomattox effectively signal the end of the conflict? Why did southerners lose the will to fight after only four years whereas the Vietnamese struggled for two generations? Late-twentieth-century realities have perhaps rendered us more ready than ever before to explore the intangible, subjective dimensions of the Confederate experience, in search of understanding rather than judgment.[6]

While the Vietnam War and changing attitudes about race in American life may have given the problem of Confederate nationalism a renewed relevance in the past two decades, they can hardly be said to have brought the issue a new clarity. Nationalism has become a part of the broader, and hotly contested, debate about the character of the Old South itself. Although Potter assumed in 1963 that the problem of a separate southern culture was all but settled in the negative, in the past three decades the influence of Eugene Genovese has brought to the notion of southern distinctiveness a new sophistication and vitality. Those who contest his assertions cite southern defeat in the Civil War as a telling datum in their arguments for persistent underlying national homogeneity. To historians such as Carl Degler, Kenneth Stampp, and Charles Sellers, nineteenth-century southerners were overwhelmingly American, even as they risked their lives to deny this inescapable identity. The common culture and values of North and South in the prewar period produced a southern nationalism that was spurious rather than "genuine"; southern defeat was both the result of and evidence for antebellum national cohesion.

Southerners, these historians contend, felt sufficiently uneasy about both slavery and Confederate independence not to fight very hard for either.[7]

The road to Appomattox is so direct in this version of events that one is left wondering why the South ventured forth on it at all. If southern nationalism is to be dismissed, how then explain the birth of the Confederacy and its willingness to fight four years of the bloodiest warfare then known to mankind? Within such a framework, the only criterion for the genuineness of Confederate nationalism would have been the achievement of southern independence. Steven Channing has posed the dilemma forcefully: "Hindsight tells some of us that secession did take place, that the Confederacy *was* created, and therefore that Southern nationalism was bona fide, with all that implies. Hindsight tells others that the Confederacy collapsed into defeat and that nationalist claims were therefore a fraud." And what hindsight tells each of us, I might add, seems to correlate closely with what we already think about the South in the prewar years. Nationalism, much debated as it has been, has become in all of this a kind of epiphenomenon; it is treated variously (or sometimes simultaneously) as an offshoot of a debate about the nature of antebellum civilization or as the occasion for a value-structured inquiry into the depths of southern commitment to slavery and the distinctive way of life it engendered.[8]

The limitations inherent in such a vision seem all the more striking in light of the explosion of recent historical work on ideology. The once widespread view that ideology should be devalued because of its so-called "cognitive insufficiencies *vis-a-vis* science" has been largely replaced by a recognition that the very subjectivity of all belief offers important insight into the motivations and meanings of human behavior. With growing interest and subtlety, scholars in the past two decades have been tracing the interactive relationship between ideas and society, endeavoring to escape the reductionism that would make either thought or objective social factors the sole determinants of historical behavior. Ideas are now likely to be regarded in and of themselves as an essential aspect of social action. Significantly, much of this work has been profoundly influenced by theories about ideology that originated in the anthropological study of nationalism. The inescapable citation in almost every historical study of ideas and culture completed within the past decade has been Clifford Geertz's

"Ideology as a Cultural System," an essay in which Geertz's own field research on Indonesia served as foundation for the more abstract discussion of ideology that captured the interest and imagination of so many historians.[9] Yet the origins of the new history of ideology in the study of nationalism have been all but forgotten. I would guess that most of the scholars who have cited Geertz's essay would not even remember that it includes a substantive treatment of Indonesian nationalism. Certainly in the case of scholarship on the American South, where Geertz's influence has been as deeply felt as in any other area of American history, few questions have arisen about the relevance of his work to the study of Confederate thought. There has been precious little in-depth examination of southern wartime ideology. Some scholars have even denied its existence. "The war did not permit sage debate by learned men about the Southern soul," Emory Thomas has written. "The pressure of time and the pace of events demanded that Confederate Southerners define themselves in deeds. Accordingly the Confederacy acted out its national identity." Yet there are Confederate words as well as deeds, and these words offer the possibility of insight into the Confederates' view of nationalism—their vision of this common enterprise and of their efforts to transform opportunity into reality through the creation of a national culture.[10]

But just as some scholars have regarded the reactive growth of the proslavery argument in the years after the rise of abolitionism as evidence of the weakness of the South's sentiments about slavery, so scholars taking note of Confederate efforts to create a national culture have often hailed these undertakings as testimony to the absence of a "genuine" nationalism, of the "mystical" and "spiritual" oneness that should have been present from the outset. Confederates had to build a culture, the argument goes, because they did not have one in the first place. Yet if we examine other nationalist movements, it is clear that the "creation" of culture has almost always been a necessary and self-conscious process. In our own century, both Nazis and Italian Fascists made determined efforts to socialize youth, indoctrinate citizens, and create common symbols in the service of national spirits that have hardly been seen as deficient in intensity. Although the manipulation of media involved in such efforts perhaps seems more suited to an age of mass culture and communication than to the era of the Civil War, it had its functional precursors in earlier eras. The

French revolutionaries, in the moment that has been seen as the birth of modern nationalism, produced symbols of political values and group solidarity designed to mobilize the masses. And recent historical scholarship has demonstrated that such nationalist staples as the Scottish kilt, tartan, and clan, or the Welsh language were far from being "genuine" defining cultural attributes based in a long-shared sense of common identity. These were inventions, adopted in a particular historical context to serve as symbols of national unity.[11]

Comparative inquiry reminds us that nationalism is more often than not "insufficient" at the time of its first expression. Nationalism is contingent; its creation is a process. It is not a substance available to a people in a certain premeasured amount; it is rather a dynamic of ideas and social realities that can, under the proper circumstances, unite and legitimate a people in what they regard as reasoned public action. Such a view of nationalism, moreover, underlines the political nature of the undertaking, directing attention to the social groups seeking to establish their own corporate ideals and purposes as the essence of group self-definition. The struggle for the achievement of nationalism often becomes itself the occasion of its fullest realization.[12]

The study of Confederate nationalism must abandon the notions of "genuine" or "spurious," of "myth" or "reality." Such approaches are equivalent to embarking upon the study of religion by inquiring into the validity of its substantive claims, or to opposing "ideology" and "truth" in order to dismiss the former as an object of analysis. Ideas are social actions, albeit symbolic ones, and they must be treated in this way as facts, analogous to any other historical data. Southern historians should be the first to recognize that myths and realities often amount, in practice, to the same thing.[13]

A detailed inquiry into the structure, substance, and process of Confederate nationalism is thus long overdue—not, however, because it will tell us why the South lost the Civil War, though it may eventually lead us closer to such understanding. We cannot break out of the circularity and sterility of most historical discussions of Confederate nationalism until we set aside this emphasis on hindsight; interpretation must precede evaluation. We must begin to explore Confederate nationalism in its own terms—as the South's commentary upon itself—as its effort to represent southern culture to the world at large, to history, and perhaps most revealingly, to its own people. Only when we have come to understand the substance and meaning of this system of belief will we be able to assess its influence on Confederate fortunes and southern history. The creation of Confederate nationalism was the South's effort to build a consensus at home, to secure a foundation of popular support for a new nation and what quickly became an enormously costly war. The formation of this new national ideology was thus inescapably a political and social act, incorporating both the powerful and the comparatively powerless into a negotiation of the terms under which all might work together for the Confederate cause. Independence and war reopened unfinished antebellum debates, intensified unresolved prewar conflicts, and subjected some of the most fundamental assumptions of the Old South to public scrutiny. In doing all this, the Confederate effort to define a national identity produced a revealing record of southerners struggling to explain themselves to themselves.

Southerners were, in fact, strikingly self-conscious about the need to undertake this introspection and to publicly define the foundations of their unity. William Bilbo, for example, called upon a Nashville audience, in the fall of 1861, to dedicate itself to exciting "in our citizens an ardent and enduring attachment to our Government and its institutions." As a North Carolina grammar text explained, "The political revolution in which we are now engaged makes necessary an intellectual one." The *Southern Literary Messenger* believed that the South badly needed to explore "the great social and philosophic truths that lie concealed" behind the dramatic events of the day. The work of the periodical press, the editor concluded, should be to formulate and disseminate just such a philosophy. The Richmond *Age* had a similar conception of its mission, intending to be "a vehicle for the conveyance of ideas, the prevalence of which we conceive indispensable to a permanent establishment of our National Independence." The Atlanta *Daily Register* proclaimed its equally bold notion of the role of the press: "We must develope [sic] sentiments . . . which catching the spirit of the age, and reflecting upon the world the true meaning of our wonderful position, *shall be aggressive upon the mind of the whole American people.*" The *Smith and Barrow's Monthly Magazine* of Richmond issued "A Plea for Monuments," urging the creation of literary as well as sculptural renditions of national symbols to serve as inspiration for "a new and holier love and zeal for the welfare and happiness of that country, which produced and gave to the world these models." The magazine itself, its editors explained, was dedicated to "placing before the people, to be seen, read and admired by all, their common property, which cannot be possessed separately and apart by each, but is made here imperishable, in a fixed and definite shape, forming a nucleus for their best love and highest hopes to cluster around." Confederate journalism became almost by definition a nationalist venture.[14]

Efforts at cultural creation were by no means confined to an elite of journalists, educators, and clergymen. The Montgomery *Daily Advertiser* urged wide public identification with the stirring events of the winter and spring of 1861. It offered a *"facsimile copy"* of Alabama's secession ordinance as an emblem for the wall of each house in the state, to be "hung side by side with the old Declaration, as a memento of the times." One correspondent, signing herself a "True Southern Woman" of Lowndes County, Alabama, wrote to the Montgomery *Daily Mail* in February, 1861, with an elaborate plan of didactically symbolic pageantry for Jefferson Davis' inauguration. Only such "due form and ceremonial style," she urged, could set the august tone appropriate to the new nation. "Demagogues and agrarians," she continued, were certain to be stymied by such an atmosphere.[15]

When a committee of the Confederate house asked for suggestions from the public for the design of the new national flag, hundreds of recommendations poured in—nine out of ten, the legislators noted, from ladies. One enterprising Virginia matron set about to create a unique "National relick" to be cherished in ages to come. With the cooperation of Mrs. Robert E. Lee, she procured locks of hair from a dozen Confederate generals and fashioned them into a sculpture that she intended to put on public display. Other patriotic southerners invested their energies in literary efforts, bombarding newspapers with so much unsolicited poetry on national themes that one publication threatened to charge the authors at the same rate it set to print obituaries. A more appreciative editor proudly greeted these "effusions" as "the veritable paeans . . . of a nation's birth hour." Ceremonies, flags, "relicks," monuments, poems, and songs—southerners clearly felt the need to create symbols of national identity.[16]

Educated Confederates were familiar, too, with the emblems of national unity identified as significant in nineteenth-century na-

"One enterprising Virginia matron set about to create a unique 'National Relick.'" Hair sculpture by J. Emma Conrad. Courtesy of The Museum of the Confederacy, Richmond, Virginia.

tionalist discourse. Southern intellectuals of the prewar period had read widely in the literature of European romanticism, and the contents of antebellum periodicals demonstrate their familiarity with such nationalist prophets as Johann von Herder, Johann Fichte, Jules Michelet, and Alphonse de Lamartine. Many of the southerners who published essays on these writers in the 1840s and 1850s became leading secessionists. David Flavel Jamison is perhaps the most notable example, for he followed his numerous periodical contributions on French and German nationalist ideas with service as president of the South Carolina secession convention in 1860. In an only half-joking charge that Sir Walter Scott had caused the Civil War, Mark Twain long ago identified the means by which many of these nationalist notions were transmitted widely among reading southerners. Scott's immensely popular Waverley novels celebrated Scottish struggles against English domination and oppression in a manner southerners found increasingly resonant with their own situation, and these volumes became soldiers' acknowledged favorites in camp libraries.[17]

Confederates drew from these sources a quite explicit sense of the attributes seen by their age to legitimate national status. "National Characteristics" were hailed by *DeBow's Review* as "The Issue of the Day." Yet the emphasis placed by European nationalist thinkers on political differentiation based on separate race, language, religion, and history was problematic for white, English-speaking southerners; to many nineteenth-century observers, as to many historians in the years since, Confederates seem all but indistinguishable from their former countrymen. The creation of a unique Confederate culture thus involved self-conscious cultivation of special features of southern national character, for these could serve as justifications for political independence.[18]

Already dependent upon racial arguments to defend the logic of their social system and their daily lives, southerners eagerly embraced the notion of a racially determined nationalism. "The original antagonisms existing between the North and the South," one author explained in *DeBow's Review,* were a "necessary consequence of their radical difference in race." The presence of "Anglo-Saxons" in the North and "Normans" in the South had made disruption of the United States inevitable—"only a question of time." The portrayal of northerners as "Saxons," descendants of the oppressive Englishmen depicted by Scott, had gained currency in the South well before the war, but in the wake of secession, it became an important rationalization for the new nation.[19] Confederates also addressed the issue of an appropriate national language. But their calls for language reform did not focus on the preservation of provincial forms or peculiar southern dialects; there was no southern equivalent of Basque or Gaelic. Significantly, southern school texts argued instead for restoring a purity of diction that would lead white southerners toward their English linguistic roots and away from both Yankee degeneracies and what the texts called "AFRICANISMS." Southerners must learn to enunciate the last letters of words. "Never say an' for and; mornin' for morning; objec' for object." Final *ngs* were a special problem, worthy of an entire chapter in one reader: "Avoid saying *readin', writin', takin', walkin', lockin' etc.*" And it was important to "sound the R's" as well: "Poor, not pooah; matter, not mattuh." Most of these errors seemed to Confederate critics directly copied from black speech. "Many a distinguished Southern orator," one school text observed, "has had to study hard before he could break himself of 'Mammy's' Africanisms." Adelaide Chaudron's best-selling reader attacked "Dis," "Dat," "Deeze year," "Bofe," "Hee-äh," and "Fum," as "grammatical 'barbarisms'" learned from slaves and requiring translation into English. The South was to be neither colony nor province; Confederate speech must be no patois, but the language of the metropolis— free of mongrelization or creolization. Just as France was struggling in this period to turn peasants into Frenchmen by creating a single, standardized national tongue, so the South would aspire to linguistic uplift and uniformity. The Confederacy was now a nation among nations; she must speak, the Charleston *Mercury* urged, no "corrupt provincial dialect, but the noble undefiled English language," a language of power.[20]

Identifying their speech with that of existing national states, Confederates similarly cast their struggle for independence as the equivalent of successful nationalist movements. The dynamic fervor of the French Revolution proved inescapably attractive to southern spokesmen, who invoked French precedents—especially martial victories—in spite of a lingering fear of the excesses into which that movement had degenerated. The "Marseillaise," published in several appropriately southern versions during the war, became one of the Confederacy's most popular songs—"the

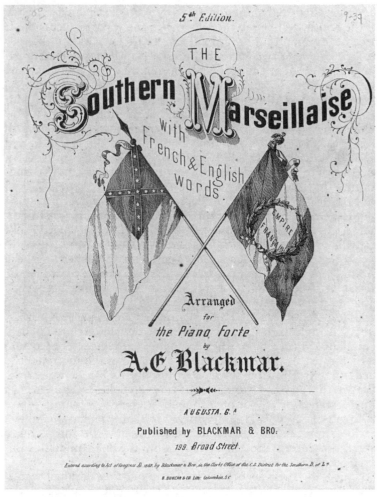

"The 'Marseillaise,' published in several appropriately southern versions during the war, became one of the Confederacy's most popular songs." Sheet music. Courtesy of the Boston Athenaeum.

rebel tocsin of liberty," one Virginia matron called it. In fact, the anthem was so completely identified with the southern cause that a troupe of French actors visiting New York was jailed as southern sympathizers for singing it.[21]

Contributors to Confederate periodicals explored parallels between the Confederacy and other fledgling nations or independence movements—the Dutch republic, the "young kingdom of Italy," and the Polish and Greek rebellions. But the authors were careful to dissociate the South from genuinely radical movements; it was the conservative European nationalism of the post-1848 period with which the Confederacy could identify most enthusiastically. The Dutch struggle, an essayist in the July, 1862, issue of the *Southern Presbyterian Review* explained approvingly, was like the Confederate, for in both situations, "not we, but our foes, are the revolutionists." The *Daily Richmond Enquirer* was even more explicit about the Poles.

> There is nothing whatever in this movement of a revolutionary, radical or Red Republican character. It is the natural, necessary protest and revolt of, not a class or order, but an ancient and glorious nation, against that crushing, killing union with another nationality and form of society. It is not the poverty, and plebeian or proletaire interest rising up against superior classes; rather it is the aristocratic and high-bred national pride of Poland revolting against the coarse brute power of Russian imperialism. . . . At bottom, the cause of Poland is the same cause for which the Confederates are now fighting.[22]

Confederate diplomats hailed the similarities between the Confederacy and other recently established states in order to claim the South's right to international support and recognition. Secretary of State Robert Toombs urged his Mexican envoy to emphasize Confederate admiration for the "triumph" in that country "of those principles of constitutional government for which the Confederate states are now battling." Mexican history seemed to him "freighted with episodes similar to that which now agitates the Confederate States." The southern government welcomed a Spanish analogy between Napoleon's invasion of Spain and northern advances across the Potomac. British recognition of the new Italian state encouraged Toombs to see parallels there, as well. "Reasons no less grave and valid than those which actuated the people of Sicily and Naples," he explained, had prompted the Confederacy to seek its independence.[23]

But the nationalist movement with which the Confederates most frequently identified was—paradoxically yet logically—the American War of Independence. A central contention of Confederate nationalism, as it emerged in 1861, was that the South's effort represented a continuation of the struggle of 1776. The South, Confederates insisted, was the legitimate heir of American revolutionary tradition. Betrayed by Yankees who had perverted the true meaning of the Constitution, the revolutionary heritage could be preserved only by secession. Southerners portrayed their independence as the fulfillment of American nationalism.[24]

Evidence of this self-image abounded in the new nation. The figure of Virginian George Washington adorned the Confederate national seal and one of the earliest postage stamps; Davis chose to be inaugurated at the base of a statue of Washington on Washington's birthday in 1862; a popular ballad hailed the Confederate president as "our second Washington." Songsters used by soldiers and civilians alike were filled with evocations of past glories such as the battles of Cowpens and Yorktown—events, like the figure of Washington himself, at once American and southern.

> *Rebels* before,
> Our fathers of yore,
> *Rebel*'s the righteous name
> *Washington* bore.
> Why, then, be ours the same.

Through identification with the War of American Independence, Confederates hoped not just to cast themselves as equivalent to the thirteen original states. They intended to claim American nationalism as their own, to give themselves at once an identity and a history.[25]

Thus from the first days of southern independence there existed a widespread and self-conscious effort to create an ideology of Confederate nationalism to unite and inspire the new nation. In many particulars, this endeavor built upon antebellum attempts to encourage southern distinctiveness: William Gilmore Simms had already rewritten the history of the American Revolution with a southern accent, and the call for southern textbooks and southern literature had been sounded for decades. But in the context of war and independence, this agenda acquired a new urgency. It no longer rested primarily in the realm of culture. The Confederacy's declaration of nationhood had, within the framework of

nineteenth-century nationalist doctrine, made culture explicitly
political, inextricably tied to the power of this new Confederate
state at home and abroad, as well as the direct concern of a now
official group of Confederate leaders. The creation of Confederate
nationalism, the establishment of a common understanding of
national identity and purpose, was a prerequisite to Confederate
survival—with or without the challenge of total war. As an Italian
nationalist leader tellingly proclaimed upon the establishment of
an Italian state in 1860, "We have made Italy. Now we must make
the Italians." [26]

But in important ways, ordinary southerners stymied the efforts
of a self-conscious elite to "make the Confederates," to impose a
coherent nationalist ideology on the South. The insistence of the
southern people upon a voice in constructing Confederate nationalism profoundly influenced both its form and content. In the
prewar era, southern slaveowners had successfully dominated the
region through their ability to elicit the consent and cooperation
of the largely enfranchised masses of nonslaveholding whites. The
notion of hegemony that has come so much into vogue in recent
years has been aptly used to describe the contingency of slaveholders' power and to underline the significance of culture and
ideology, as contrasted with naked force, to their social control.
The South's ruling class had to make a persuasive case for its
authority—a case that necessarily changed with the advent of
independence and war. New state sovereignty, new responsibilities, and new demands placed upon the people required renegotia-
tion of power within the South. Defining the terms of national
unity became the occasion for examining its fundamental conditions. Slaveholders moved rapidly to shape this discussion in their
own interest, for nationhood was itself a creation of this interest—
of the dominant class's effort to protect its cherished way of life
from the challenge of American national control. [27]

Yet within the structures of southern politics and southern society, the ruling class could not act in its interest alone. Confederate nationalism had to win popular assent if the Confederate nation was to survive. The terms of southern nationalist ideology
were thus profoundly shaped by these two, often countervailing,
forces: first, the purposes of the ruling class; and second, the rhetorical role of nationalist thought, a body of ideas designed, as
William Bilbo put it, to "excite in our citizens an ardent and enduring attachment to our Government and its institutions." The

loudest voices in the Confederate South were still those of the powerful; an elite of planters, clergy, politicians, and intellectuals led the movement to create a shared public culture and to produce consent to the terms of its rule. The formulation of Confederate ideology was, in large measure, an attempt to make class interest synonymous with national interest. Yet the effort to persuade a majority to identify with a cause that most directly served the class interest of a minority required some accommodation of non-slaveholders' concerns. In the way of all hegemonic systems, therefore, Confederate nationalism became a hybrid of elite purpose and popular influence; it was an ideology intended to serve as a basis for widespread social and political consensus.[28]

At the same time, Confederate nationalism was formed by the limits of the possible. As a public ideology, it had to be publicly available. Yet the prewar South had relied largely on northern publishing houses and printing technology, and wartime conditions intensified the difficulties of communication within the region. Confederate nationalism cannot be understood apart from some consideration of how it was shaped by the means available for its dissemination. As Benedict Anderson has recently emphasized, nationalism requires that a group of strangers imagine themselves intimately related to one another. "An American," he writes, "will never meet, or even know the names of more than a handful of his 240,000,000-odd fellow Americans. He has no idea of what they are up to at any one time. But he has complete confidence in their steady, anonymous, simultaneous activity." This confidence, this imaginative power, was first made possible by the spread of printing and literacy beyond a restricted upper class to an extensive public, which consequently came to share a sense of cultural community through its common experience of newspapers and popular literature.[29]

Many Confederates certainly recognized the critical role of the printed word. The editor of the *Southern Literary Messenger*, for example, explicitly linked the success of the southern nation to an enhancement of the role of print within the region. "Like all people much given to talking," he wrote, "Southerners, as a people are little given to reading. Our education . . . is derived chiefly from conversation and verbal discussion. . . . We can never become profound in either thought or education until this superficial habit . . . shall be supplied by some more durable form of instruction." Southerners must, for their survival, become "more of a reading and less of a talking people."[30]

The South's difficulties in communication arose not only from its orality and its comparatively lower levels of literacy. Its lesser technological development in comparison with the North inhibited its effectiveness in the wars of the mind as it did on the field of battle. The South had only one typefoundry, no facilities for printing maps, insufficient numbers of paper mills, and an entire inability to make wood-pulp paper, which began to gain importance in the North after 1863. "With no small feeling of chagrin, and some of shame," the *Southern Monthly* noted in 1861, "we are forced to confess that a well-illustrated magazine *cannot* yet be produced in the South. Good artists we can procure, but good engravers on wood are scarce among us." There was no engraver in the Confederacy capable of rendering the new national seal; it had to be made abroad and run through the blockade. So, too, when a new southern school text became widely popular, an agent had to be sent to Edinburgh to have it stereotyped, for adequate facilities no longer existed within the South. Nor were there adequate means to disseminate what was produced. "Unfortunately," *DeBow's* observed, "the people . . . are not sufficiently supplied with book agencies and other facilities for the extensive distribution and diffusion among themselves of the works of their own writers." The Confederate mails did little to ease this problem. Confederate postal rates were two to three times higher than those of the United States. Davis was sufficiently insensitive to the implications of this reality that the Confederate Congress had to pass a bill to provide free mailing of newspapers to Confederate soldiers over his veto. By the later years of the war, mail service in Richmond had broken down almost entirely, with hundreds of thousands of undelivered items piled up in the city post office.[31]

The problems of distribution steadily increased. When Nashville fell, the South lost its only stereotyping facility. Type wore out and could not be replaced; paper shortages mounted as paper mills were destroyed and rags became ever scarcer. Merton Coulter has estimated that only 14 percent of Virginia's newspapers continued to publish after 1862; in Mississippi it was only 12 percent. If printed media enable citizens to imagine national communities, the South had a problem from the outset—a problem that intensified with each year of conflict.[32]

The implications of these structural realities for Confederate nationalism are numerous. For example, anything published and disseminated in the initial months of the war had a far greater potential impact than information made public after the severe restraints of war had been imposed on the southern media. Confederate nationalism was thus inhibited in its ability to grow and change. What was said initially is what was heard most widely. What could be spoken as well as read, moreover, was likely to have greater impact. The South's limited literacy combined with problems of distribution and supply to ensure a wider audience for oral than for printed genres. This, of course, poses significant methodological dilemmas for the historian, who has no access to the spoken record of the pre-electronic age. Yet oral creations, or at least versions of them, were often preserved in some sort of written form. Sermons were printed or summarized in manuscript notes; songs were published as well as sung.

Wartime music is the most striking example of the importance of southern orality in the creation of Confederate nationalism. The production of songbooks and sheet music outstripped every other area of southern publishing during the war, expanding dramatically in response to popular demand. A multiplier effect also operated to increase the effect of each printed sheet. Songs were more often than not sung in groups, which are, as Benedict Anderson has noted, the "physical realization of imagined community." Individuals learned words by rote and passed them on. For those at home or in camp who lacked direct access to the printed song sheets, memory often sufficed.[33]

Anthropologists have long recognized the importance of meter, rhythm, and rhyme in the communication of oral tradition in preliterate cultures. In the South, song lyrics were transmitted in much the same manner. One young woman from Baltimore, who had just run the blockade into the Confederacy, was the guest of General P. G. T. Beauregard in his Virginia camp. Serenaded by his troops, she responded with a rendition of "Maryland, My Maryland," a ballad as yet unknown in the South. The soldiers took up the refrain and learned it on the spot; the song soon became a favorite within the army and the southern nation at large.[34]

This ease of dissemination, requiring no access to editors, printing presses, or binderies, made song a logical medium for direct popular expression. The *Daily Richmond Enquirer* perhaps overstated the case when, in an 1862 editorial, it proclaimed war songs to be "the spontaneous outburst of popular feeling" showing "the sentiments of the people" and giving the "lie to the assertion of our enemy, that this revolution is the work of politicians and party leaders alone." But numbers of songs were written by ordinary southerners—especially women—in remote locations throughout the South, and many well-received ballads stimulated direct popular responses, creating a kind of singing dialogue throughout the South. "Rock Me to Sleep, Mother" was a favorite among soldiers, who found their anxieties echoed in the song's plea for an escape from war back into childhood, even if just for a single night. One infantryman responded to a chorus of the song, offered by his comrades just before battle, by applauding its sentiments and asking that as long as he was to be made a child again, it be a girl this time. Another ironic variation, devised at "Camp Mud Hole" in Tupelo, Mississippi, was entitled "Exempt Me from the War." "Forward, march forward old time in your flight," it urged. "Make me too old to be in the next fight." A more formal rejoinder, published as a best-selling song in its own right, sought to counteract the rather dangerous ambivalence about combat that "Rock Me" represented. From heaven, the mother reassures her frightened son that he need not fear death; he need not escape into childhood, or anywhere else, should the dishonorable thought occur to him.

> Could you but see thro' this world's vale of tears
> Light would your sorrows be; harmless your fears
> . . . .
> Follow me cheerfully; pray do not weep
> In spirit I'll soothe you, and "Rock you to sleep."[35]

A number of Confederate songs served almost as catechisms in civics for the far-flung southern public. In the early days of conflict, every victory was imprinted on the southern mind by an appropriate ballad. Bethel, Manassas, Sumter—each became a song title. Some Confederate, either too callous or too patriotic to think better of it, even composed a "Pickets [sic] Charge March." Every successful general had his own song or songs, serving as mnemonic devices in the creation of the newly inaugurated Confederate history. And not only military figures were so honored. Jefferson Davis appeared in a number of titles, and there was even a "Mason and Slidell Quickstep" to honor the Confederate diplomats captured by the Yankees. One is compelled to observe that their steps were evidently not quick enough.[36]

In considering the problem of Confederate nationalism, I have been using *problem* in several somewhat different senses. The first sense is historiographical: the obstacles to understanding that have arisen from presentist political and moral considera-

"Every successful general had his own song or songs, serving as mnemonic devices in the creation of the newly inaugurated Confederate history." Sheet music. Courtesy of the Boston Athenaeum.

tions. These have prevented us from examining Confederate nationalism on its own terms, as a system of meaning within its own context.

The second sense is the way in which Confederate nationalism posed itself as a problem to Civil War southerners themselves, thereby influencing the nature of the nationalist ideology they endeavored to create. From the start, Confederate nationalism was self-conscious. The building of national unity, like the creation of a winning army, was a problem southerners had to meet. Their efforts to forge a sense of common identity were, in turn, shaped and constrained by a set of inescapable realities—problems in a third sense of that term. Comparatively low literacy levels and the weakness of the region's publishing and printing industries caused difficulties in disseminating ideas—difficulties that in one way or another affected every attempt at national communication, influencing the form in which it appeared and the impact it was likely to have.

The content of Confederate ideology, not just its form, was also shaped and constrained by its situation. Southerners' understanding of nationalism as a nineteenth-century political philosophy and as a form of political legitimation profoundly affected the way they conceived of their own undertaking. At the same time, the realities of power distribution in the South dictated that Confederate ideology be at once elitist in purpose yet popular in appeal, a condition that became increasingly difficult to meet. As an essential part of this production of consent, Confederate nationalism had to reassure the South of the conservatism and continuity of its revolution; it had to draw upon existing systems of meaning, long-cherished bodies of thought and legitimation, to minimize the perception of upheaval and change caused by secession and war. Confederate nationalism had to cast independence as the logical outcome of all that had gone before, using the available repertoire of ideas and beliefs to reassure southerners that their new departure was, in reality, no departure at all.

Some political theorists have suggested that nationalism is always about the struggle between tradition and modernity. An inquiry into Confederate ideology can provide only a relevant test case. Yet the way in which many powerful and articulate southerners endeavored to reconcile their revolution with tradition, to have change without change, becomes the story of Confederate nationalism, and perhaps of the Confederacy itself.

"A Nation to Do His Work upon Earth": Religion, Politics, and Confederate Nationalism

The most fundamental source of legitimation for the Confederacy was Christianity. Religion provided a transcendent framework for southern nationalism. During the antebellum period, southerners had portrayed themselves as the most godly of Americans, and independence and civil war only reinforced this identification. Few Confederates would have disagreed with the journalist who insisted that "we are really the most religious people in the world." This claim to divine blessing represented not just a deeply held conviction but a sound ideological strategy for an evangelical age, a posture designed to win support both at home and abroad. Day-to-day realities of southern life worked as well to make religion central to the new nation. In a region where evangelical commitment was at once widespread and profound, the authority of the clergy at least rivaled that of the new Confederate state, for preachers possessed in their weekly sermons one of the most effective and influential means of reaching the southern population. The war, as the *Southern Christian Advocate* noted, represented "a remarkable and much to be coveted occasion for the pulpit to assert itself as a power in the land." Patriotism was "to be wedded to piety, and . . . God's ministers are to perform the service," one clergyman exulted. "Never before in our history," the Episcopal bishop of Texas alerted the ministers of his diocese, "has such an opportunity been afforded for the Church to appear in her true relations to the State."[1] But Christianity was not simply the servant of the Confederate state. The doctrines of Christian evangelicalism had an inescapable logic of their own, one that came to pose threatening dilemmas within the realm of Confederate thought. In embracing religion as a central foundation and legitimation for their movement, Confederate nationalists sought to strengthen their cause before the world and their own people. Yet the prominence of Christianity in Confederate culture and identity ultimately worked in unforeseen and contradictory ways.

Confederate Christians confronted one dilemma almost immediately. Even though they hailed the initial bloodless victory at Sumter as clear evidence of God's favor, southerners soon recognized that independence would cost thousands—even hundreds of thousands—of human lives. From the time of Augustine, thinkers have struggled to reconcile the carnage of war with Christian teachings. But for almost fourteen hundred years, what has come to be known as the just war tradition evolved largely as the province of theologians, jurists, and philosophers, who legitimated war as an institution yet worked through church and crown to limit the occurrences and the intensity of organized conflict. With the emergence of nationalism in the eighteenth century, however, notions of *jus ad bellum* took on new manifestations and new significance. Fueled by the growing political importance of popular ideologies, nationalist movements transformed just war theory into public discourse, a source of authority and legitimation not only for kings, but for entire peoples. The mass mobilization of men required a parallel mobilization of ideas.[2]

To the soldier who, like one Texan, feared participation in battle as "the most . . . blasphemous thing perhaps on earth," the need for spiritual reassurance was imperative and immediate. As a Baptist chaplain declared to Charleston's Moultrie Guards in 1861, a citizen soldier must "first of all" be "thoroughly persuaded of the justice of the cause to which he devotes his life." Sermons, tracts and religious newspapers distributed in the ranks—even popular songs—addressed the question that had initially troubled Augustine so many centuries before. Did man possess an ethical right to engage in combat, or was war inherently antithetical to Christian teachings? In an attempt to answer this question for Savannah's Pulaski Guards, Bishop Stephen Elliott invoked an argument that echoed the formulaic phrases of the religious defense of slavery. "Is there anything in the Gospel," he asked, "which forbids a Christian man from bearing arms and fighting in his country's service? We unhesitatingly answer, that there is nothing; no shadow of a prohibition where the war is defensive." The Old Testament was full of godly warriors; and in the New, John the Baptist reassured soldiers of their righteousness; Christ never assailed the profession of arms; and early Roman Christians served readily as soldiers. "The military life," Elliott concluded, "seems to have been treated by Christ as was every other department of domestic and social arrangement." In the interludes between sermons, songs and tracts offered similar reassurance. "Our cause is just and far dearer than life," echoed one popular march. "Their's [sic] must be the guilt," proclaimed another. A widely circulated pamphlet assumed the form of the traditional catechism, urging the soldier himself to recite and thus reinforce his belief: "*I am here,* because I believe that *defensive* war is justifiable. . . . The present war, is on our part, emphatically a war of defence; and would not lose its *defensive* character, even if . . . we should find it necessary to advance into the very midst of the enemy's territory."[3]

Just as the Civil War extended beyond the battlefield to involve the whole southern population, so an understanding of the war's origins and purposes had to be communicated to civilians as well as soldiers. "Upon the intelligent conviction that we are right," the *Biblical Recorder* observed in 1861, "must depend the fervor of our prayers for the success of our arms, and our confidence in the establishment of our institutions." In part, this effort at persuasion assumed familiar political and constitutional forms, recapitulating the arguments for southern rights that had issued from the halls of Congress and the pens of southern editors for at least three decades. Jefferson Davis' presidential messages were filled with assertions of the South's legal right to secede, to determine its own form of government, to protect its property and way of life. As one Confederate congressman intoned as late as 1865, "This is a war for the *constitution,* it is a *constitutional war.*"[4]

Yet, as the Confederate choice of national motto clearly indicated, the new nation consistently sought profounder justification. Beneath George Washington's image on the national seal appeared the words "Deo Vindice," an epigram selected by the Confederate Congress to express "the religious sentiments of the

"Beneath George Washington's image on the national seal appeared the words 'Deo Vindice,' an epigram selected by the Confederate Congress to express 'the religious sentiments of the nation.'" The Great Seal of the Confederacy. Courtesy of The Museum of the Confederacy, Richmond, Virginia.

nation. " In his repeated calls for God's aid and in his declaration of national days of fasting, humiliation, and prayer on nine occasions throughout the war, Jefferson Davis similarly acknowledged the need for a larger scope of legitimation. Nationhood had to be tied to higher ends. The South, it seemed, could not just be politically independent; it wanted to believe it was divinely chosen. The Confederacy, the *Christian Observer* stated in 1862, "will be the Lord's peculiar people"; it would be, a fast-day sermon proclaimed, the "nation to do his work upon earth." Beginning with an evocation of well-established tenets of just war doctrine, the Confederacy's claim to divine sanction extended beyond the question of the war's origins or immediate political purposes to an examination—and reevaluation—of the southern social and moral order in light of God's commands. The purpose of the war, as southerners explained it in the course of these inquiries, was not simply to achieve independence, but to defend the moral right of survival for the South's peculiar civilization.[5]

Such transcendent notions were far from new in American politics. From the time the Puritans embarked for New England, belief in a divinely chartered errand had motivated New World settlers. The creation of American independence in 1776 did not interrupt, but incorporated and reaffirmed, these traditions. National politics were intimately tied to religion in what one scholar of the revolutionary era has called a "convergence of millennial and republican thought." The Confederacy self-consciously portrayed itself as the fulfillment of this legacy, and the wartime fast day became a recurrent occasion for clerical solemnization of this marriage of the sacred and the secular. Proclaimed by the state and celebrated by the church, the fast day possessed a political and theological rationale that gave it multivocal significance. The time had arrived, as one minister explained, when "the claims of moral and political duty are so indissolubly connected, that they cannot be considered apart."[6]

Jefferson Davis' invocation of the tradition of public fasting, humiliation, and prayer represented the South's symbolic claim both to God's special favor and to an important component of the American heritage that the Confederacy now sought to make its own. Religious fast days, focused around sermons of humiliation and self-doubt, had made their first New World appearance not in the South but among New England Puritans. From these origins, the fast day and its characteristic jeremiad of self-scrutiny became, as Perry Miller and Sacvan Bercovitch have described, an American national ritual. Just as the South explicitly cast itself as the legitimate heir, rather than the destroyer, of the Constitution and the Revolution, so in the use of the jeremiad, the Confederacy implicitly identified itself with American tradition. The biblical language of providential selection that had inspired the seventeenth-century Puritans and the patriots of 1776 now defined Confederate purposes. Whereas the North had perverted these ideals, the South had seceded in order to preserve what would otherwise be lost. Secession represented continuity, not discontinuity; the Confederacy was the consummation, not the dissolution, of the American dream. A sermon preached in South Carolina explained the nature of the South's relationship to this history. "I have heard men in their ignorance," Alexander Sinclair reported, "attribute our national disorders to the influence of Puritan doctrines. Egregious error! The doctrines of the original Puritans were, and are, the doctrines of the Bible. . . . But the descendants of the Puritans have gone far astray from the creed of their forfathers [sic]." Confederate independence, explained a Methodist tract quoting Puritan John Winthrop, was intended to enable the South, "'like a city set upon a hill' [to] fulfill her God given mission to exalt in civilization and christianity the nations of the earth." [7]

Identification with these components of American nationalism necessarily involved transcendent purposes, and the enormous and unexpected scope of the war made such legitimation all the more imperative as the conflict entered its second, third, and fourth years. "To shed such blood, as we have spilled in this contest," Stephen Elliott declared in 1864, "for the mere name of independence, for the vanity or the pride of having a separate national existence, would be unjustifiable before God and man. We must have higher aims than these." Creating Confederate nationalism thus came to involve more than simply establishing a new political status for the South; it required the location of the Confederacy not only within the world but within eternity, as an instrumental part of God's designs. All "nations," an 1861 fast-day sermon explained, "have their assigned missions." A nation should not be a "dead abstraction, signifying only the aggregation of individuals"; instead, it "possesses a unity of life . . . analogous to the powers of . . . will in a single mind. It stands in definite moral relations." The Confederacy could not simply be the political embodiment of a people sharing certain common characteristics or beliefs; there was a dynamic aspect of its national self-definition that required the new state to actively seek fulfillment of its eternal mission. Confederate nationalism had necessarily to prescribe future behavior as well as describe present reality. The elaboration of this larger mission thus became central to the new nation's evolving understanding of its identity, and the clergy central in defining Confederate national purpose. Independence and war had created—as symbolized in the simultaneously sacred and secular moment of the fast day—a new temporal, even political, relevance for the church and its spokesmen. "A pure Christianity," a Greensboro minister declared, "is wrapped up in this revolution, and Providence is using the South for the grand work of its preservation and extension." Confederate nationalism subsumed the evangelical fervor of Confederate Christianity.[8]

The assumption that underlay such a sense of mission and structured the fast-day ritual was the existence of a covenant between God and a particular people, a reciprocal agreement that offered a nation God's special favor in return for adherence to a particular national version of his larger design. This conception of covenant, it is important to emphasize, implied not so much that southerners as individuals were special; instead, it signified that they were *corporately* special in a way that rendered religion and nationalism inseparable. Such an ideology transformed God himself into a nationalist and made war for political independence into a crusade.[9]

The possibility of salvation on a level even more exalted than that of individual justification offered a powerful nationalist appeal within an evangelical South, encouraging Christians to embrace the corporate identity that would bring them to such realization of God's grace. Fast-day jeremiads established a history—and a legitimacy—for nationalism that stretched back not just to 1776, but to the Hebrews. The tribes of Israel had made the first secession; the name of God's first chosen "Chief Magistrate," one minister explained, was remarkably like that of his current designate. "David broke off from the first Israel under the reign of the house of Saul. . . . Davis broke off from the second kingdom of Israel under the reign of her first King, A. Lincoln, and established the second kingdom of Jerusalem." The Reverend J. Jones, addressing the Light Guards of Rome, Georgia, in 1861, was only one of many preachers throughout the South to choose as his text the striking first chapter of Jeremiah. "Then the Lord said unto me, out of the North an evil shall break forth upon the inhabitants of the land, and they shall fight against thee, but they shall not prevail against thee; for I am with thee." Not all southern clergy invoked quite such ingenious biblical analogies, but a great many used the fast-day occasion to emphasize that Old Testament events seemed "wonderfully exact in their parallelism to events happening around us to-day." Sacred and secular history, like religion and politics, had become all but indistinguishable. In the early months of independence, many clergymen voiced delighted surprise at the discoveries of correspondences between the southern situation and a wide variety of biblical events. The analogy between the Confederacy and the chosen Hebrew nation was invoked so often as to be transformed into a figure of everyday speech. Like the United States before it, the Confederacy became the redeemer nation, the new Israel.[10]

The reciprocity between God and his chosen thus obligated southerners as a group. The everyday concern of southern churches was individual salvation, but the regular employment of the fast day during the war years implied other sorts of duties that especially concerned southerners as a people and a nation, that defined them by specifying their particular relationship with God. As the Montgomery *Daily Advertiser* stated, the fast day represented "a National acknowledgement of God's intercession in behalf of our cause." Yet the continuing tribulation of war made clear the failure of the chosen people to carry out their covenanted obligations. War, the southern clergy recognized, was one of God's hallowed instruments in the correction of states. A Virginia fast-day sermon explained, "While individuals look forward to a judgment and a world to come, nations, as nations, have no existence in another world—their retributions and punishments are meted out and suffered in this."[11]

In the attempt to explain what Confederate ministers, like their Puritan predecessors, often called "God's Controversy With Us" and in order to interpret the crisis at hand, the wartime jeremiad scrutinized southern society with a critical severity rarely seen before the war. Antebellum southern religion had been characterized by an emphasis on personal morality as the key to salvation. In contrast to many of their northern counterparts, southern evangelicals had shied away from advocating fundamental structural or institutional transformations in society. Emphasizing the need for individual moral uplift rather than widespread social change, southern reformers strove to avoid the dangerous "isms"—feminism, socialism, abolitionism—that had emerged from northern efforts at social betterment. As a result, the proliferation of reform movements that spread through the rest of nineteenth-century America did not take as firm a hold in the South. But the logic of Confederate nationalism, with its notion of corporate mission, was to prescribe significant shifts in the southern definition of Christian duty. Mounting adversity threatened, the *Religious Herald* declared, "to become more and more potent in ascertaining what the [national] character is, even with respect to the deficiencies which have heretofore slept undeveloped in the bosom." Assuming that "*all* calamities, in whatever shape they come, are the result of sin, and are either judgments for it or admonitions to repent," southern clergy set out to identify the region's shortcomings. Only a reformation could stay the punishing rod. "When we become what we ought to be," Baptist minister Henry Tucker declared in a fast-day sermon to the Georgia legislature, "there can be no motive in the divine mind to continue the chastisement, and the war will cease."[12]

Southerners had at least taken the first step in their regeneration by separating themselves from the sinful North. The United States had consistently violated the terms of its national covenant. Those ideals and purposes that had originally won the special favor of God had all but disappeared in a haze of corruption and degeneracy. "There is no instance upon record," Bishop Elliott proclaimed in 1862, "of such rapid moral deterioration of a nation as has taken place in ours in the last forty years." Secession thus became an act of purification, a separation from the pollutions of decaying northern society, that "monstrous mass of moral disease," as the Mobile *Evening News* so vividly described it.[13]

The vision of the jeremiad, and its focus on decline, almost perfectly paralleled the influential antebellum political ideology of republicanism, with its assumption of a lost world of public virtue and its calls for redemption through a return to past values. These sermons thus helped to provide the Confederacy with more than just a means of claiming the religious dimensions of American nationalism as its own. In the jeremiad, the South identified itself as the true heir of the republican tradition as well. Although in religious discourse this purpose most often remained implicit or metaphorical, it was occasionally stated explicitly. "Let us strive," urged one fast-day sermon, "to bring back the purer days of the republic, when honest merit waited, like Cincinnatus at his plow, to be called forth for service."[14]

The notions of corruption and degeneracy served the Confederacy well in another sense, permitting the South at once to assume the mantle of American nationalism and to dissent from it. Honoring Americanism in the abstract, as a set of ideals for which the nation once stood, Confederates could and did assail any number of actual United States policies and attitudes as declensions from the original standard. The sins for which war was serving as punishment, a grammar school text explained, were partly "our sins, and partly . . . the sins of our forefathers." Sabbath-breaking, for example, seemed to many southern clergymen a blasphemous violation of God's designs and "one of the sins which has, in a measure, come down to us by entail from the Federal Government." A more general national unwillingness to make structural and institutional acknowledgment of God appeared a certain source of chastisement. Confederates took great pride in the specific invocation of God in their own constitution, in contrast to the "Godless instrument" still in effect in the North. "May it not be," Charles Colcock Jones, Jr., asked his father, "that God is now punishing this nation . . . for this practical atheism and national neglect in not by organic law, legislation, and in a public manner acknowledging his supremacy?" Presbyterian leader James Henley Thornwell took the effort yet a step further in his attempt to win specific constitutional recognition of Christ. The problem with the United States Constitution, he explained, was that it endeavored "to make the people a God."[15]

The American nation, many southern clergymen argued, had neglected God not just in the formulation of governmental charters but in the most fundamental operations of national political life. The error that underlay most of America's sins was the development of doctrines that, as Reverend Calvin Wiley put it, "glorify man, and as a natural consequence, discredit God." It was imperative, Georgia's Methodist bishop George Foster Pierce urged the Georgia general assembly, to "talk less of the rights of the people and more about the rights of God." Here the Confederate jeremiad invoked divine sanction for political reaction, a rejection of the democratizing tendencies of the post-revolutionary years in favor of an earlier era when virtue—and privilege—reigned. Republicanism had a conservative potential that had long appealed to many elite southerners, who saw in the doctrine of rule by the virtuous a rationalization for their continuing power. Within Confederate nationalist ideology, such attitudes found new opportunity for expression, now in close alliance with the most elitist tendencies within the southern clergy. In "obedience to His will," a Texas Episcopalian explained, "there is ever . . . a virtuous subjection!"[16]

In their struggle to build a southern ideological consensus that also served their own designs, members of the southern clergy could thus appeal to two touchstones of mid-nineteenth-century American, and especially southern, belief: republicanism and evangelicalism. But the particular use to which these notions were put in the southern jeremiads demonstrates the protean quality of the ideologies themselves. Depending on the interpreter, republicanism and evangelicalism could be reactionary or progressive in implication, elitist or democratic. The key to their success as the foundation of hegemonic ideology lay in making them seem to be both at the same time—or more precisely, in creating images and references that would be constructed in predictably different ways by different social and political groups.

In the Confederate jeremiad, the challenge of war and independence led at least some southern clergymen to voice more open calls for social and political reaction than they had previously dared. In time of national crisis, doctrines of "spirituality" that had restricted engagement in terrestrial affairs could be justifiably set aside. Religious and political duty became all but inseparable. Although ministers were remarkably skillful at interweaving the designs of God with the more mundane purposes of the republic, they were less successful at maintaining the balance between elite and democratizing ideological tendencies within each of the two areas of thought.[17]

The South should relearn, one clergyman urged, "the virtue of reverence—and the lesson of respecting, obeying, and honoring authority, for authority's sake." Man was ultimately incapable of self-government, the argument followed, and must be controlled by God's discipline. Only those with explicit belief in a future state of reward or punishment could be trusted to act virtuously. Democratic political forms thus inevitably subverted God's purposes. "Many are the national evils which we brought with us," a Virginia Presbyterian minister warned. "The first step in this process of recovery requires *a modification of the law of universal suffrage."* A political pamphlet published in 1862 echoed these sentiments, with the same mixture of political and religious concerns. Hailing God as "the blessed and only potentate," the essay "specially urge[d] the Confederate Government not to persist in the maintenance of the democratic theory." Even Jefferson Davis expressed concern about the heretical arrogance implicit in the widespread southern assumption that men had the right and the power to determine their own fate. In a fast-day proclamation of late July, 1863, when Gettysburg and Vicksburg had brought a dramatic turnabout in Confederate military fortunes, Davis mused whether our "successes . . . made us self-confident and forgetful of our reliance on Him."[18]

The need for the southern people to acknowledge God's authority was bound up with a legitimation of the authority of both clerical and civil rulers. Christian humility became identified with social and political deference as the clergy urged submission to both God and Jefferson Davis. "The preachers of the Gospel in the South," the *Confederate Baptist* reminded its readers, "have from the beginning of the struggle for independence, devoted their energies to the support of the government. . . . [W]hile Congress has resounded with declamations of which the President or his Cabinet was the theme, the ministry, without exception have remembered him in their public prayers, and exhorted their flocks to sustain the country in its season of trial and peril."[19]

The antidemocratic rhetoric that issued from many southern pulpits had its direct political parallels, suggesting the relevance of these clerical pronouncements as both influence and legitimation in debates concerning the distribution of power within the new regime. This was an ideology closely related to immediate political needs. Powerful southerners hailed independence as the occasion for a return to a lost republic of virtue in order to justify their calls for a variety of reactionary measures that they sought to define as essential parts of Confederate identity. As the *Daily Richmond Enquirer* observed, "One often hears Confederate citizens expressing distrust of the permanency of Democratic institutions in this country; sighing for gradations of rank, hinting that 'the mob' ought not to rule." This struggle over the social and political meaning of independence represented the culmination of a half century of constitutional controversy. Within individual states, first the revolutionary heritage of liberty and then the national impact of Jacksonian democracy had offered significant impetus for the democratization of governmental charters to widen suffrage; to subject more offices, including judgeships, to popular election; and to equalize forms of taxation. The coming of war and of Confederate independence interrupted this movement, creating a situation in which new realities implied new options and dictated new tactics, both to those advocating and to those resisting increased popular control.[20]

The summoning of state conventions set the stage for these conflicts in two ways. The assembling of supralegislative bodies created the need for widespread political consensus on secession and other issues. Yet, in many states, the conventions also provided the opportunity for an oligarchy to take advantage of the crisis to advance its own antidemocratic ends in the process of state constitution-making that followed withdrawal from the Union. Most historians have tended to focus so exclusively on the secession debates of these bodies as to all but forget that they were also charged with amending the state constitutions to conform to the new political order. In an important sense, the secession conventions defined the Confederacy—not just in establishing its political independence, but by specifying the terms of a new civil order in each state. Their significance lies in what might be called their metapolitical status; they self-consciously set out to articulate political goals and purposes for the new nation.

While some conventions took their constitutional mandate to mean little more than removing references to the United States from existing documents, leaders in other states seized the opportunity to remake state charters in accordance with what they perceived to be appropriate ideals for the new nation—ideals that, when made explicit, often bore strikingly reactionary implications. The tensions between populist gestures and elitist tendencies within these bodies shed considerable light on the political character of the Old South, suggesting that the region possessed neither a fundamentally "democratic" nor an essentially "aristocratic" nature. Instead, southern politics rested in a carefully balanced equilibrium that, thanks in large part to black slavery and widespread antebellum prosperity, provided a measure of satisfaction for southern whites of all social classes. But with the advent of war and of the inevitable sense of political opportunity inherent in changed circumstances, many ruling-class southerners anticipated strategic advantage in challenging this equilibrium on behalf of their own particular political goals.

Ordinary men, on the other hand, recognizing first that their votes were necessary for secession and later that their bodies were required for battle, sought reforms in taxation, governmental structures, and public services that had been denied them in the prewar years. As Governor Joseph Brown explained this war-born symbiosis, Georgia's slaveholders "are dependent upon our white laborers in the field of battle, for the protection of their property; and in turn, this army of white laborers and their families are dependent upon the slave owners for a support while thus engaged."[21]

But it was the elite that more effectively interjected its concerns into the public discourse of Confederate nationalism. These individuals were far more likely than inhabitants of western Virginia or of the North Carolina mountains to have means to reach the public at large, through either print or oratory. Just as the clergy called for an end to the people's presumptuous disregard of the appropriate terrestrial and divine authorities, many conservative southern politicians similarly saw 1861 as the moment to reverse the democratic tendencies that had rapidly gained momentum within the United States since the turn of the century. Like the clergy, these public voices endeavored to associate despised popular innovations with Yankee degeneracy and moral—not just political—error.

A fundamental issue in states that debated extensive constitutional revision was the right of secession conventions to exercise such responsibility. Opponents of convention actions argued that their assumption of the right to revise constitutions was arbitrary and oligarchic. Although theoretically the bodies may have had such power, their critics charged, the people had intended the delegates to rule on secession and nothing more. Conventions that engaged in lengthy constitutional debate, like those in Alabama, Arkansas, Virginia, North Carolina, South Carolina, and Georgia, were especially vulnerable to accusations of usurping rights that properly belonged to legislatures accountable to the people. One Alabama delegate, for example, warned that convention actions had become "directly subversive of civil liberty"; and the convention president spoke openly of the widespread popular fear that "in the exercise of the unlimited power confided to us, we might betray the people and establish a monarchy" or "remain in perpetual session, ruling over the liberties of the people." In South Carolina, the oligarchic tendencies of the convention were particularly extreme, for through the establishment of an executive

council, it presumed to become an equal participant with the
governor in the ongoing administration of the state. By spring,
1862, protest meetings in a dozen districts throughout South
Carolina were calling for the convention to adjourn sine die. In
nearly every state, the conventions exercised some purely legislative functions, citing wartime emergency as justification for these
irregularities. Convention delegates across the South invoked war
pressures again to rationalize their opposition to submitting secession ordinances and, later, the state and Confederate constitutions themselves to popular ratification.[22]

The issue of the "sovereignty" of these conventions is an in-
triguing one. The political philosophy most influential in shaping
the South's progress toward independence had been that of John C.
Calhoun. In his *Exposition and Protest* (1828), published during
an earlier moment of sectional crisis, the South Carolinian had
argued that a convention called to consider secession was, unlike
a representative legislature, the embodiment of the people themselves. Such a conception implied that the convention's powers
were not delegated but actual, and thus essentially unlimited.
Individuals defending Confederate state conventions against
charges of usurpation invoked such arguments in a remarkable
rhetorical sleight of hand. By defining the convention as "the people," it was possible to make an oligarchic body appear in democratic guise. Reaction concealed beneath a cloak of democracy
offered a potentially ideal resolution to the wartime dilemmas of
hegemony.

The Confederate state conventions demonstrated their conservatism in a number of substantive ways. In the course of both state
and national constitution-making processes, Confederates considered restricting citizenship as one means of controlling access
to political power—and keeping it in the hands of genuine southerners. Virginia, Alabama, and North Carolina, for example, debated limiting citizenship to the native-born or those who had
resided in the state for at least twenty-one years. In Alabama,
opponents of the provision attacked its reactionary implications,
speaking eloquently against the introduction of class distinctions
based on differing citizenship status among whites. "Let there be
but two classes of persons here—the white and the black. Let
distinction of color only, be distinction of class." Otherwise,
"white people will be divided into a lower and higher class . . .
promotive of constant conflicts." The proposed citizenship legis-

lation threatened to sow "the seeds of aristocracy." The Florida convention considered forbidding any United States citizen from ever becoming a citizen of Florida, or from holding real estate or practicing a profession. With the adoption of the Confederate constitution, these state discussions and provisions became moot; but heated controversy had arisen over naturalization laws at the national level, as well. These debates represented a consideration—and ultimate rejection—of one Confederate strategy to preserve the status quo. They demonstrated both the power and the limits of reaction in defining the terms of the Confederacy's ideological agenda.[23]

Convention delegates sought similar ends in their efforts to reverse many of the democratic innovations that had been made in state constitutions in the late antebellum years. Historian Michael Johnson has characterized the actions of the Georgia convention as an attempt to "circumscribe democratic practices with institutional reforms" in order to create a "patriarchal republic." The reduction in the size of the legislature and the shift of supreme court and superior court justices from election to appointment represented a reversion to an earlier constitutional era in Georgia and enhanced, Johnson has argued, the power of individuals like the convention members themselves. In North Carolina, delegate Thomas Ruffin argued before the convention that "above all times this is the one . . . to give the people a sound conservative constitution." His judiciary committee recommended the institution of new property qualifications for some offices and the removal of other offices entirely from popular control. The Alabama Committee on the Constitution also recommended abandoning election of superior court judges, arguing that "nothing was more . . . destructive of our confidence in the people of the North, than the fact that judges, elected by the people, and the mere instruments of popular prejudice, would soil their ermine . . . because their robes were placed on their shoulders by the votes of a fanatical people." In Arkansas as well, judges were now to be appointed by the governor, rather than elected, as they had been before the war.[24]

Perhaps the fullest expression of such sentiments appeared in Virginia. In November, 1861, a committee appointed to consider constitutional revisions called for a restriction of suffrage to taxpayers and a reduction in the number of popularly elected local and statewide officials. These changes, the committee members argued, would effect a return to the true and forgotten underpinnings of the American experiment. "It cannot be denied," the committee insisted, "that it is in violation of one of the great fundamental principles of American liberty that persons who pay no taxes should be allowed to exercise the elective franchise." Western delegates, however, effectively resisted a committee effort to vest the election of the governor in the legislature, and the convention also determined to make curtailment of suffrage a separate proposition. Nevertheless, the convention presented to the people a constitution far less democratic than that which had been in force for the past decade, for it sharply reduced the number of elective offices and established a judiciary largely independent of the people.[25]

Almost all convention delegates, as well as newspapers representing the entire political spectrum, agreed that the 1850–1851 democratization of the Virginia constitution had gone too far toward institutionalizing erroneous Yankee political notions within the state. In the mixed language of religion and politics so characteristic of Confederate treatments of these issues, the Richmond *Whig* hailed the reformist efforts of the convention as "A Deliverance from Yankeeism," and a Staunton paper urged voters to "complete our redemption from Yankeeism." The Richmond *Daily Dispatch* urged approval of a constitution freed from the "Yankee innovations" of the old and expressed its conviction that the first alteration of Virginia's 1776 charter had marked the "beginning of our descent to an abyss from which nothing but this great revolution can save us." Richmond editor and humorist George Bagby wrote only partly in jest when he reported in a dispatch to the New Orleans *Crescent* that changes were being made in the Virginia constitution "in anticipation of the political millennium which is to dawn on Old Virginia the moment she is free from the thralls of Yankee-diddle-daddle-doodledom."[26]

Bagby's summary of the convention's actions is illuminating, for he acknowledged the continuing sense of need to compromise, to maintain the equilibrium of democratic and hierarchical tendencies, even after the departure of much of the western portion of the citizenry into the new Union state of West Virginia. "The spirit of the Virginia Convention is willing," he wrote, "but the flesh is too weak to accomplish the reforms needed in the Constitution, and to restore the admirable structure given to us by the fathers." To ask soldiers to reenlist after their initial twelve-month term at almost exactly the same moment as removing their right to vote seemed counterproductive, one delegate argued convincingly.[27]

But in terms of our concern with ideological strategies, the crucial issue is less the substantive political outcome than the dialogue that preceded actual political decisions. Proponents of reaction recognized war-born opportunities at the same time they confronted new wartime social and political constraints that influenced both what they said and how they said it. This was nationalism in creation—not a preconceived body of theories or abstractions, but ideas as rhetorical weapons, useful insofar as they could persuade, legitimate, or inspire. The forceful assertion of conservative doctrines as at once southern and sacred and the hegemonic effort to equate Yankeeism simultaneously with democracy and the Devil profoundly shaped the character of Confederate nationalism as it was promulgated from the pulpit, the stump, and the press. Those southerners who had embraced hierarchical political and social views in the antebellum years seized upon the changing situation as an occasion to advance these views and to associate them as closely as possible with the ongoing process of national self-definition.

The reactionaries in one sense had the ideological upper hand, for not only did they have better access to southern media, but their case made for a better fit with the political posture that had traditionally been seen to distinguish the North and South. But at the same time, practical realities made the southern elite more dependent than ever before upon the white masses who filled the ranks of the Confederate army. The spirit of reaction was compelled to cloak itself in the forms and appearances of democracy. Issues like suffrage restriction would paradoxically be submitted to popular vote; conservatives urged the people to affirm their willingness to surrender political power. As one delegate embroiled in the conflicts within the Alabama convention explained in urging submission of the secession ordinance to the people, "We want harmony among ourselves. This, sir, is of so much importance to our success, that, so far as possible, it ought to be secured." The conservative tendencies within Confederate nationalism were profoundly altered and attenuated by the need to negotiate consensus, creating troubling paradoxes at the heart of

Confederate identity. Contradictions that had long existed in southern life were inevitably sharpened; the rhetoric of reaction was becoming more militant and more explicit at the same time that the power of the masses was growing dramatically as a result of their new military indispensability.[28]

"Sliding into the World": The Sin of Extortion and the Dynamic of Confederate Identity

God had sent war as a scourge and chastisement to reform his erring people; the South had to repent of her sinful ways to stay his corrective discipline. As Presbyterian leader James Henley Thornwell warned his fellow Confederates: "Dependence upon Providence carries with it the necessity of removing from the midst of us whatever is offensive to a holy God. If the government is His ordinance, and the people His instruments, they must see to it that they serve Him with no unwashed or defiled hands." The definition of Confederate identity within such a religious framework made reform central to Confederate national purpose. The punishing blows of war demonstrated that the status quo was not good enough. Even though secessionists had hoped to forestall rather than foment a revolution, the ideology of southern independence made it clear that military victory would not be achieved without significant moral and social change.[1]

The enumeration of the Confederacy's most egregious transgressions was an important undertaking, for it involved the negotiation of a public consensus about those areas of southern life that seemed most seriously awry. In the effort to define Confederate sins southerners themselves identified the Achilles' heel that they believed threatened the new nation with a critical vulnerability.

Although Confederate jeremiads invoked a wide range of short-comings as justifications for God's wrath, two sins came to hold unchallenged preeminence in Confederate religious and political discourse, serving as subjects not just for fast-day sermons, but legislative initiatives, popular literature, and newspaper editorials. Anxieties about what Confederates called "extortion," or greed, and unease about the operation of their peculiar institution rivaled southern distress at lengthening casualty lists and dwindling supplies of men and materiel.

From the time of their first rationalizations of secession in the winter of 1860–61, southerners had been citing the growing materialism of American, and especially northern, society as a fundamental justification for Confederate independence. The seemingly unbounded prosperity of the American nation had corrupted the republican virtues of its politics, while "Mammon-worship" had undermined the spiritual foundations of religious life. "We have been *victims of prosperity,*" the Reverend Charles Cotesworth Pinckney proclaimed to his congregation of wealthy Charlestonians in February, 1861. Bishop Thomas Atkinson of North Carolina agreed, declaring a few months later: "Great prosperity has been the ruin of many countries, and of many men in every country. It has surely been the occasion of a large part of our present miseries." Office-seeking, ambition, selfishness, and greed threatened the survival of the republican political order at the same time that, a prominent southern Methodist affirmed, "the Church has been sliding into the world." Southerners charged that northern influence had given material values undue prominence, for Yankees were by nature, a Confederate school geography text explained, a "keen, thrifty, speculating. . . people; money-loving and money making, without much restraint as to means, *success* being the all-absorbing object." A popular rhyme entitled "Yankee-Doodle-Doo" turned from description to condemnation, proclaiming a "Curse on the canting, whining race, / The peddling, meddling crew." By freeing the more naturally spiritual and generous southern character from such pernicious influences, nationalists argued, Confederate independence would help bring an end to this alarming process of moral degeneration.[2]

In seizing upon such arguments, secessionists once again turned to the venerable traditions of the religious jeremiad and the political doctrines of republicanism. Prosperity, and consequent corruption, had been focal points for New World sermons since

Puritan lamentations of moral decline in the seventeenth century. Similarly, republican ideology had from the earliest days of the new nation warned of the threats to liberty posed by the temptations of American wealth. Except for its use to justify secession and to imply southern moral superiority, such rhetoric was neither new nor peculiarly southern; it traced its American origins back nearly two hundred years.[3]

But the designation of "extortion" as a cardinal American sin had special meaning for southerners of 1861. At the culmination of a decade of high cotton prices and remarkable economic growth, much of the region was in the midst of dramatic commercial expansion. At a number of points throughout the South, this dynamic posed significant challenges to a traditionalism that had generally proved more tenacious within the southern social and economic order than it had in the northern.

While the North had moved rapidly in the early decades of the nineteenth century toward commercial and capitalist development, the South had remained largely rural and agricultural. Slavery had profoundly inhibited the growth of market relations in the region, both by preventing the emergence of a free market in labor and by limiting the number of the section's independent consumers. Many nonslaveholding white southerners remained largely autonomous producers, relying for most of their needs on the yield of their own farms rather than entering into extensive dependence on market transactions. The profits and prosperity of the 1850s, however, brought profound change to much of the South. The lure of commercial staple agriculture proved irresistible to many small farmers. State governments began to encourage market development in a number of ways as well, most notably by subsidizing transportation improvements. In Georgia, industrial capital doubled during the decade, as did railroad mileage and the annual value of industrial production. In South Carolina, railroad investment increased three and one-half times in the same period. The place of the market in southern life had begun to change even before the Civil War directly challenged the system of slavery that dictated the peculiarities of the traditional southern way of life. American ambivalence about prosperity, and the particular rhetorical forms this uncertainty had so long assumed, thus had a special resonance within the region as secession approached.[4]

After 1861, the South was forced to confront these contradictions in the context of a transformation even more dramatic than that of the 1850s. Wartime inflation, shortages, and economic dislocations provided a rich environment within the Confederacy for the growth of just those excesses of greed that secessionists had identified as peculiarly northern. Economic mobilization required new levels of southern industrialization and development and devastation of crops and livestock forced many formerly self-sufficient agriculturalists into the grip of inflationary wartime markets. Thousands of southern men experienced wage labor for the first time as soldiers in an industrialized war, and women, too, entered the labor force in unprecedented numbers.

The prominence of the sin of extortion—or crime of extortion if one chooses the political rather than the religious framework of discussion—in the public rhetoric of Confederate self-examination and definition represents an attempt by southerners to explore the meaning and control the impact of these changes in southern life. Ironically, even though Confederates greeted independence as a means of resisting the incursion of market values and materialism into southern life, the war caused by secession all but doomed that effort.

Initially, southerners expected that war, like secession, would loosen materialism's tightening hold on the South. War was, a Richmond Presbyterian clergyman explained in 1861, one of God's means to "show that there are nobler things to be contended for in life than mere material advancement." The dislocations of military conflict, a Georgia Methodist agreed, were certain to "arrest the corruption of prosperity—to unsettle, agitate, break loose the people from their plans and hopes—dethrone their *cotton idol*" so that once more God could truly be king. Even Lincoln's oppressive blockade of southern ports promised to have the salutary effect of checking the "extravagance" that had for years been "swelling . . . among our people."[5]

In spite of such sanguine expectations, southern clergymen continued to focus on avarice as one of the Confederacy's most troubling national sins. And circumstances quickly brought this concern into the secular realm of national discourse. Evidence of God's displeasure as expressed in the brutal chastisements of war combined with war-generated material temptations to focus Confederate attention on what was soon recognized as a growing, rather than shrinking, preoccupation with gain. No longer simply the subject of church sermons and republican orations, greed became in the Civil War South a central theme of Confederate popular culture. Plays, novels, poems, children's school books, and Sunday school weeklies all addressed the problem while Confederate and state legislatures struggled to find an appropriate governmental role in containing the unbridled pursuit of wealth. As the Montgomery *Daily Advertiser* observed, "The whole country is ringing with denunciations of the extortioners."[6] Increased wartime demand and the shortages generated by the movement of thousands of agricultural producers into military service disrupted existing patterns of self-sufficiency and supply throughout the South. As in most wartime economies, the opportunities for profiteering were rife, and many southerners eagerly took advantage of the new possibilities for wealth and social mobility. One Confederate army officer observed the scene in Savannah. "The social changes that progress with the revolution are many . . . ; the rich are ruined, the poor grow rich; some of the best property in this City . . . has been purchased by German Jews, who were lately the poorest of the poor. Anyone who is willing to buy, keep, and re-sell at a profit can grow rich; the recipe is simple." There were, an Episcopal clergyman noted, "PECULIAR AGGRAVATIONS AT A TIME LIKE THE PRESENT" to the age-old sin of avarice; Baptists, too, found themselves lured by the "seductions of the times." The more general prewar concern about greed thus came by mid-1861 to focus specifically on the essentially interchangeable sins of extortion and speculation, the manipulation of wartime shortages and exigencies for personal profit.[7]

Both clergymen and lawmakers sought to define this evil more precisely in the early months of conflict. The *Central Presbyterian*, which ran a series of articles on the topic, stated explicitly that *"extortion is the demand of high prices, from the poor, for the necessaries of life, without a proportionate cost in their production."* Such a formulation emphasized the introduction of an inflationary and illegitimate stage between production and consumption, an unjustified intermediary market action that severed price from value. In a similar effort at definition, Bishop Alexander Gregg of Texas noted that extortion implied "a disposition to go beyond the bounds of a *just and lawful gain.*" But here the bishop referred to neither state nor even denominational law; instead he cited more transcendent, less precise notions of the Mosaic code and the "eternal laws of rectitude."[8]

Legislators confronted grave difficulties in translating such abstract principles into enforceable ordinances. A bill to "prevent speculation, hoarding and extortion" was read twice before the Confederate senate but was reported adversely by the Committee on the Judiciary, which regarded its implementation as problematic and feared it would dampen motivation to produce badly needed goods. Confederate president Jefferson Davis appealed to individual states to pass measures to "suppress the shameful extortion now practiced upon the people by men who can be reached by no moral influence," and the debate moved to the state capitols. The Virginia legislature devoted extensive consideration to the matter over a period of more than a year, discussing several different bills and convening hearings that included interviews with manufacturers. A fear, like that expressed in the Confederate Congress, of inhibiting production, and a sense of inability to frame an act that would prove effective, prevented Virginia's senate and house from agreeing on an ordinance. Seven states, however—Florida, North Carolina, Texas, Georgia, Alabama, South Carolina, and Mississippi—did pass measures against extortion and speculation, but in many cases, even they regarded the legislation as symbolic rather than regulative. Only nine months after passage of Georgia's law in 1861, Governor Brown ruefully admitted it had become a "dead letter."[9]

However ineffective and unenforceable these measures may have been, they nevertheless served as important statements of public values. Their specific content embodies the Confederate understanding of extortion as well as of the proper operation of the market. The laws focused on excessive prices, especially for "breadstuffs" and other necessities, and on market manipulations, such as hoarding and "forestalling," that might cause price inflation. The ordinance passed by the North Carolina convention in November, 1861, one of the earliest of such measures, made the same value-laden distinction between the activities of production and of marketing as had the *Central Presbyterian*. In a section of the act designed to prevent individuals from creating monopolies in order to increase prices, the convention declared an extortioner or speculator to be one who, with the intention of reselling, "shall engross or get into his hands, by buying, contracting, or other means, except by producing, corn" or other "present necessities" of the people. Some states specifically designated a particular percentage of profit—75 percent in one South Carolina Senate bill—as the maximum allowable, but others relegated to a jury the determination of "exorbitant or unreasonable rates or prices."[10]

This reliance on juries—embodiments of general community values and opinions—harks back to Bishop Gregg's invocation of "eternal laws of rectitude." Southern notions of just price seemed to exist in a realm beyond and above the law. Price represented in many southern minds a platonic ideal of worth independent of market operations. It was the interference of the wartime market with these abstractly "just prices" to which southerners objected; markets had rendered extrinsic and mutable what southerners had previously regarded as intrinsic values. Instead of inhering in the good itself—in the product and the value of the producer's labor —price had now become an artifact of the market. The growing popularity of the auction, with its implicit rejection of any notion of fixed or "just" price, appeared the ultimate embodiment of these pernicious tendencies, and Virginia, for example, even considered legislation to prohibit auctions altogether.[11]

But such perceptions could not easily be translated into positive law. "Human legislation," Bishop Gregg admitted, "will strive in vain to correct the evil. . . . To those divine instrumentalities which he has graciously set on foot for the moral renovation of mankind, must we look in faith, as the only effective and final remedy." Public exhortation was certainly one such instrumentality, and clergymen regularly chose to address the problem of extortion in their lamentations on Confederate sinfulness. Church councils, too, considered the best means to combat the evil. The Baptist *Religious Herald* suggested prayer as the appropriate remedy; and the Presbyterian Synod of South Carolina, like the Evangelical Lutheran Synod of Virginia, appointed a committee to "investigate the subject." The secular press devoted extensive attention to the problem as well. George Bagby, editor of the *Southern Literary Messenger* and Richmond correspondent to newspapers all over the South, began listing as examples "Worthy of Imitation" the names of merchants donating supplies to the poor or charging soldiers well below market rates for necessities. The Lynchburg *Virginian* offered its readers 136 lines of poetry detailing the many outrages committed against all segments of the southern population by wartime profiteers and concluding with a blasphemy rarely seen in print in the God-fearing Confederacy.

So, with this prayer, this ballad ends,
That an All-just Creat[or]

> May bless the soldier and his friends
> And damn the Speculator.

Nor were children spared disquisitions on the subject. "The boys and girls," the monthly *Children's Friend* warned, "have caught the spirit, and many of them, we fear, are becoming eager speculators." New Confederate school books offered similar admonitions.[12]

Perhaps the most extended popular treatment of the issue appeared, however, in a novel. Published in 1864, Alexander St. Clair Abrams' *The Trials of the Soldier's Wife: A Tale of the Second American Revolution* explores the tragic fate of a young matron left in New Orleans to care for her two children after her husband's departure for battle. Compelled by the vicissitudes of war to become a refugee, she finds herself at the mercy of a series of extortionate merchants, who cheat her out of her meager possessions and leave her and her children to starve. Driven by the need to buy medicine for her sick daughter, Mrs. Wentworth steals a small purse filled with money from one of the merchants who cheated her. Tried for her crime, she is pardoned by the judge upon the appeal of her husband, who returns on furlough from the front.[13]

This moral tale offers Mrs. Wentworth mercy. But it does not go so far as to legitimate her resort to theft in the service of a morality higher than that of the marketplace; there is no suggestion that the money she has stolen was rightfully hers, as some sort of restitution for the funds extorted from her. Although she is not jailed, the medicine she purchases with her ill-gotten funds is ineffective, and her daughter dies. Mrs. Wentworth herself is so overcome by her tribulations that she goes mad and soon joins her child in another world.

Heartrending as this account is meant to be, its author is too ambivalent about his subject to move beyond sentimentality to genuine political or social criticism; there is no challenge to the market forces that have made this tragedy possible. The novel concludes its "sad commentary on our patriotism" with a call for charity, a means of mitigating, but not fundamentally altering, the operations of Confederate economic life. "This book," its author writes, "is an appeal to the Rich in favor of the Poor." Even the greed of the extortionate merchant Swartz, Abrams concludes, might have been "overlooked and pardoned, had he shown any charity to the suffering poor." The novel cries out on behalf of the needs, but not the rights, of the disadvantaged.[14]

During Mrs. Wentworth's trial, the curious address of the judge to the landlord who threw the woman and her children into the streets makes these complexities explicit. Mr. Elder, the judge proclaims, "has displayed the spirit of the extortioner" and "has acted a worse part than a murderer." Yet, he continues, "I say nothing against him for doing so, for it was an indisputable [legal] right of his" to act as he did. This bifurcation of moral and statute law over the meaning of extortion in the Confederate South was not confined to works of fiction; it was a persistent theme in the arguments of those opposing legislative action against extortion. As one Alabama lawmaker summarized: "The miser is as much entitled to the protection of the law, as your large-hearted man. We may indulge a private contempt for the Shylocks, and a corresponding admiration for the large-hearted men of the land, but the law must make no distinction." This acknowledgment of two separate standards embodied the new nation's fundamental ambivalence about the rapidly changing place of the market in its social and economic life.[15]

The Trials of the Soldier's Wife exemplifies several other aspects of Confederate national discourse about extortion, particularly in its representation of the various players in the drama. Blacks, excluded by law from the marketplace in most southern states during much of the antebellum period, are virtuous innocents, retaining the traditional virtues of Christian charity, free from the seductions of greed. It is an old mammy who opens her home to Mrs. Wentworth and her children after their eviction by the evil Elder, and it is another woman slave who facilitates Mr. Wentworth's reunion with his wife.

The villains, by contrast, are white, but they are not native southerners. The extortionate merchant Swartz is described as a Dutchman, and the landlord, Mr. Elder, is of German origin. Author Abrams makes clear that many native southerners have also been drawn into the "vortex" of extortion, but in choosing to portray outsiders as his leading examples of the phenomenon, Abrams follows the proclivities of many of his compatriots.

Throughout popular discussions of extortion, Confederates bewailed the general participation of the South in the sins of speculation and avarice; yet at the same time they often fixed upon aliens of one sort or another as the primary offenders. Although Abrams does not identify his villains as Jews (his name perhaps suggests why), much of the southern discussion of extortion lapsed into anti-Semitism. Confederate congressman Henry Foote, one of the most notorious bigots, proclaimed that nine-tenths of all traders throughout the Confederacy were Jews and that "the end of the war would probably find nearly all the property of the Confederacy in the hands of Jewish Shylocks." The *Daily Richmond Examiner* was particularly assiduous in fostering views that helped to create the climate for some tragic expressions of prejudice. The best-known and probably largest scale incident of this sort took place late in the summer of 1862, when gentile residents of Thomas-ville, Georgia, expelled all the town's Jewish families, accusing them of extortion, speculation, and counterfeiting. In response to such excesses, Richmond rabbi Maximilian Michelbacher devoted a fast-day sermon in March, 1863, to attacking extortion as a nationwide—not exclusively Jewish—sin and to pointing out the many economic and other sacrifices Jews had made for the Confederate cause.[16]

The *Southern Illustrated News* perhaps indicated the limits of Confederate toleration, offering a defense that Jews might have preferred to do without. In an 1863 article entitled "Extortioners," the popular periodical declared:

> All the odium of this ruining the country and its finances has, amid great hue and cry, gotten up for a purpose, been cast wholly on Jews and foreigners. Undoubtedly they have done their share in the work. At the same time, what else could be expected from a Jew but money-getting? It is his business in life. . . . But it is susceptible of demonstration, that those complained of on all sides, *as a plague,* comprise fellow-citizens who are native to the soil . . . Gentiles in short, who have out-jewed the Jews in pulling to pieces the Confederacy, and amassing wealth thereby.

Given their essential character, in other words, more should be expected of southerners; in their preoccupation with profit and wealth, they were being untrue to themselves. One fast-day sermon on extortion was explicit. "Fighting against Yankee tyranny and oppression, we are practising Yankee cunning and heartlessness with Yankee veneration for the almighty dollar!" Confederate nationalism, here in the form of invocations of Confederate national character, served to legitimate southerners' discomfort with the emerging role of the market in their society.[17]

The extortioners in *The Trials of the Soldier's Wife* share yet another characteristic with the villains of Confederate public discourse: they are men. As a minister observed to his fast-day congregation, this sin was located among the *"male* population." The Danville *Register* in a telling article entitled "The Contrast," claimed there could no longer be any doubt that women were "the better part of creation," for while men across the Confederacy were vying for the most extortionate and illicit gains, "merciful" and *"patriotic"* women could be seen everywhere "casting their watches, their jewelry and other valuable articles into the public treasury . . . looking only to the deliverance of their country from the hands of their enemies." Confederate statesman Howell Cobb thought he understood at least a part of the reason for this striking difference. Women, he explained to a Macon audience in 1864, recognized their Christian duty more clearly than did their husbands and brothers; they were more concerned with feeding children and families, and less preoccupied with profits. Women, he might have said, were less involved in the world of the marketplace; their domain was still primarily the household. As one Georgia wife wrote her husband about the emergence of women as shopkeepers after their husbands had been called off to war, "It looks funny in Dixie to see a lady behind the counter, but it would be natural if we were in Yankeedom as it has always been the custom there." Like black slaves, women had, through their subordination, been kept in the more traditional sphere of southern life. When war forced many of them into contact with the market, as refugees from the war-torn countryside or as wives unable to produce a subsistence with their soldier-husbands gone from the farm, they entered this new world as consumers: like Mrs. Wentworth, the victims, rather than the perpetrators, of extortion.[18]

Gentiles against Jews; men against women. Extortion was dangerous not just because it was a sin in God's eyes; it also introduced alarming fissures amid a people whose survival depended upon unity. "The spirit of covetousness," a Methodist clergyman warned in 1863, "arrays the producer against the consumer, the rich against the poor, the people against the government. In times like these," he insisted, "the prevailing spirit of covetousness assumes a political character . . . becomes a political or civil crime." Extortion assumed such significance, southern spokesmen recognized, because it exposed and exacerbated the realities of class that the hegemonic ideology of the planters was dedicated to conceal. "This sin," a North Carolina Presbyterian admonished, "is punished by the conflict it produces between different classes of society." Extortion undermined the very assumptions on which southern society claimed to be based; it introduced among southern whites that very dependence and powerlessness so "dangerous to republican liberty."[19]

Extortion turned the once-stable social order upside down—"new-forms it just like a social earthquake," one newspaper observed. The opportunity for quick gain made it possible, editorials and sermons warned, for individuals with no previous social claims to advance rapidly to positions of wealth and consequent prominence. Many members of the plantation aristocracy who did not participate in this relentless pursuit of profit now found themselves at the mercy of those they considered lesser men. "The war has, in many instances," a journalist noted in 1864, "made great and sudden revolutions in the condition of the rich and poor."[20]

The accuracy of this perception of dramatic social shifts in the Civil War era has been the subject of a great deal of historical debate in recent decades. But for our purposes, the correctness of the observation matters less than the widespread fear of social revolution that it embodied. To oppose extortion was to defend not only traditional economic values but a traditional social order as well.[21]

By 1863, the radical political costs of extortion were becoming clear. Believing in the justness of pre-market values and the illegality—according not so much to positive law as to Bishop Gregg's "eternal laws of rectitude"—of the prices they now had to pay for life's necessities, a number of southerners took matters into their own hands. In cities and towns across the South—Augusta, Columbus, Savannah, Atlanta, Milledgeville, Mobile, Raleigh, Petersburg, Salisbury, and most notably, the capital city of Richmond—citizens turned to violence to procure the goods the market denied them. The majority of these rioters were women, who looted stores in Richmond until authorities threatened to use guns against them; seized supplies at pistol point from Jewish merchants in St. Lucah, Georgia; assaulted railroad depots in quest of salt; and committed "Female Highway Robbery" in Monroe County, Georgia, where twenty-eight protesters armed with guns and knives hijacked a load of cloth en route from the factory.[22]

There can be few clearer examples of what E. P. Thompson called the "moral economy of the crowd." The "breakthrough," he

"In cities and towns across the South . . . citizens turned to violence to procure the goods the market denied them." *Southern Women Feeling the Effects of Rebellion and Creating Bread Riots.* From *Leslie's Illustrated Newspaper*, May 23, 1863.

wrote in a now-classic article, "of the new political economy of the free market was also the breakdown of the old moral economy of provision." Under wartime market pressures, the southern paternalist ethos was faltering—in some cases unable, in others unwilling, to accept accustomed obligations. The scale of need required the replacement of personalistic structures of assistance—a planter's assumption of some degree of responsibility for the welfare of his lesser neighbors—with more systematic relief measures. As an angry and eloquent "SOLDIER'S WIFE" wrote to the *Daily Southern Guardian,* the "Planter" had failed to meet his obligations to soldiers' families, and the state must now intervene. "While charity," she explained, "must of course be left to private discretion, there is a higher duty to be performed, in opening the granaries of our country to consumers that their sad and pressing necessities may be relieved." But legislative attempts to enforce paternalistic values and to mitigate the effects of the marketplace represented significant change because of their very formality and their transfer of control from the planter to the state, and at least some southerners regarded such measures as a pernicious departure from older ways. Speaking in opposition to a bill in Congress to aid families of indigent soldiers, William Lowndes Yancey asserted, "The operation . . . of such a law would be partial, unequal, unjust, and of an agrarian tendency," representing "a legal discrimination in favor of the poor against the rich."[23]

Southern rioters used the same terms as Thompson's eighteenth-century English protesters. The women of St. Lucah, Georgia, proclaimed that "they were suffering & must have provisions & clothes" and that their husbands were off fighting for the merchants' freedom, while the storekeepers remained "back at home speculating off their family." If justice was not done, the protesters threatened, their husbands would not just lay down their guns and desert, but would come home "with gun in hand & their [sic] would be more blood shed than was at Bunker Hill." Explaining that she had repeatedly and fruitlessly applied for relief, a participant in the Savannah disturbance handed out printed cards defending her actions. "'Necessity,'" she proclaimed, "'has no law, and poverty is the mother of invention': . . . these shall be the principles on which we shall . . . stand. If fair words and fair means will not do, we will try what virtue there is in stones."[24]

On the first anniversary of the famous Richmond bread riot, a soldiers' paper that would have been read by many of the husbands of these desperate women editorialized on what it called "distributive justice." "Unrelieved suffering," it proclaimed, "asserts an absolute right to what is necessary for its removal." This was the logic of legitimation used by the rioters themselves.[25]

Public spokesmen condemned the rioters' choice of means with near unanimity. At the request of the secretary of war, the Richmond press, for example, censored reporting of the April, 1863, disturbance, lest others be encouraged to emulate Richmond's enterprising women. Nevertheless, a public debate took place within the Confederacy about the justness of their ends. The discussion embodies those very imperatives of political and moral economy that Thompson describes as characteristically in conflict at moments of shifting economic values and realities. Prominent Georgia journalist Joseph Addison Turner, for example, attacked the widespread preoccupation with the notion of extortion and defended the general appropriateness of existing prices. "Our press have sown dragon's teeth in their ceaseless, inane ravings about speculation and extortion . . . thus leading our people to believe that all high prices constitute speculation and extortion."[26]

Discussion in the Richmond press of the anti-extortion measures under consideration in the Virginia legislature constituted perhaps the fullest statement of the case against regulation. The *Daily Richmond Enquirer* stood firm against any governmental intervention in the market, arguing that "the law of supply and demand" must prevail. Avarice and speculation were even to be admired, for as the paper approvingly quoted one legislator, "Patriotism may do much, but the love of gain does much more" in ensuring supplies of crucial goods. A series of articles appearing in the *Central Presbyterian* in 1863 went even further to develop reasoned objections to the popular outcry against extortion. The author defended the "intrinsic justice" and "supreme authority" of the market price. Extortion, the essays argued, was a term too loosely used in the Confederacy. "High morality may deceive itself in these important matters." The seller had a right to higher prices than "in ordinary times," for "the Providence which brings both prosperity and adversity upon all men has given him an advantage, which he has a right to use but not to abuse." Insisting upon the absolute right of the operations of the market to set price, the author then demonstrated his persisting Christian sentiments by urging that some form of assistance be provided for those who encountered hardship.[27]

But such positions evoked harsh dissent, and the press acknowledged the unpopularity at the same time it defended the wisdom of its stance. One of the most eloquent—and to Confederate leaders most alarming—statements urging laws against extortion came from a mass meeting of Richmond workers and mechanics, who gathered in October, 1863, to urge support for a price-control bill before the Virginia legislature. The *Daily Richmond Enquirer* regarded the actions of this group as nearly equivalent to the bread riots of the preceding spring. The workers' declarations represented a thinly veiled "threat of mob violence." The resolutions of the meeting do reveal a level of self-conscious and articulate political radicalism unmatched elsewhere in the Confederate South. These laborers seem to have embraced the labor theory of value, the same principles of artisan republicanism that inspired many northern working-class movements of the same period.

> Awakened to a sense of the abject posture to which labor and we who labor have been reduced . . . we will not sleep again until our grasp has firmly clenched the rights and immunities which are ours as Americans and men. . . . As freemen we abhor and detest the idea that the rich must take care of the poor, because we know that without labor and production the man with his money could not exist, from the fact that he consumes all and produces nothing. . . . It is the duty of the Government to take care of the unfortunate and not the rich.

These workers had moved beyond a cry for charity, or for a reinvigoration of paternalism, to demand subsistence as a right—one they believed could be enforced by price legislation. Regulation of the forces of the market—intervention into the laws of supply and demand—represented, they argued, the only means of preserving basic social justice; the market must not be allowed to obliterate essential human values.[28]

For many clerical opponents of extortion, it was this very abandonment of moral choice that seemed to be at the heart of the matter. Presbyterian clergyman J. W. Tucker of Fayetteville echoed the themes of countless fast-day sermons, as well as the resolutions of Richmond's workingmen, when he insisted to his congregation that "the moral sense of society" took precedence over the laws of the market and represented man's volitional control over the operation of economic forces. "Does the law of demand and supply fix prices and regulate trade?" he asked. "Evidently not. If it did, man, in trade, would lose all moral agency. . . . There could be no more morality in buying and selling than in the flow of the river or the fall of an earthquake."[29]

Yet religious leaders were far from unanimous in their stance on the issue. The *Central Presbyterian* was not alone in its 1863 defense of the market. Evangelical principles simultaneously pointed southerners in two opposing directions on the extortion question. Either could be plausibly defended as consistent with prevailing religious assumptions. Modernizing impulses within evangelical thought stressed the central importance of the individual in relationship with God, challenging the organic social and moral values fundamental to anti-market thought. Yet at the same time, the humanitarian and corporate tendencies within southern religion, the centrality of the notions of evangelical stewardship and paternalism, encouraged the charitable urges of clergymen calling for price controls. These countervailing tendencies within evangelicalism created the foundation for a fundamental paradox within Confederate ideology. The issue of extortion dramatized for Civil War southerners one of the profoundest contradictions of their social world. The lure and logic of the free market directly challenged both the political economy and morality of a slave society. Slavery depended not only on the restriction of the market in labor power. It rested as well on an ideology of paternalistic obligation and authority fundamentally at odds with the notion of a laissez-faire world. The problem of extortion thus crystallized a dilemma at the heart of Confederate identity, baring contradictory urges within southern society as well as within the moral order that gave the movement for Confederate independence its meaning.

IV

"God Will Not Be Mocked": Confederate Nationalism and Slavery Reform

To many Confederates, the preeminence of market over human values seemed responsible for a southern betrayal of divine trust still more egregious than extortion. "The love of money," a Florida clergyman explained to his fast-day congregation, "is the governing passion with us, and so the planters as a class have not pursued that course which would have stopped the mouth of [abolitionist] fanatics. . . . When the primary thought . . . is, the pecuniary investment of planters and the continuous production of calicoes, it cannot be expected that the moral sympathies of men should be enlisted in favor of the institution. . . . Had we been governed in our conduct towards servants by Christian principles . . . the moral sense of the world would have been with us." For all the prominence Confederates gave extortion in fast-day sermons, legislative discussions, and the secular and denominational press, they did not regard it as the most flagrant of the new nation's sins. Nor did they hail the cleansing separation from Yankee materialism as the most important justification for southern independence. Instead, in public discussion of both the war's origins and its purposes, southerners repeatedly cited slavery as a fundamental source of sectional conflict and a foundation for their peculiar national identity.[1]

Curiously, historians have tended to understate the importance of slavery within southern consciousness during the war. In part, this may be because in postbellum decades many southerners themselves disavowed slavery as a major cause of the conflict. Like former Confederate vice-president Alexander Stephens, they instead stressed political or constitutional considerations, which seemed more palatable, even honorable, after emancipation had become a *fait accompli.* And recent scholarly work, while in many cases emphasizing the institutional importance of slavery, has not fully explored its place within the more subjective realm of Confederate thought. Paul Escott's 1978 study of Jefferson Davis, for example, emphasized the Confederate president's relegation of the slavery issue to a "subordinate position" within Confederate ideology, and Michael Johnson has advanced a similar interpretation of secessionists in Georgia. There has been little treatment of the ideology of slavery within the Confederacy, even though during the war years, many Confederates, like Alexander Stephens himself, hailed the peculiar institution as the new nation's "corner-stone." And scholars have neglected as well the way in which popular culture echoed the concerns of these official spokesmen. Historians have focused on the joint disintegration of slavery and the Confederacy, rather than on the role of slavery in the formation of Confederate national identity. Jefferson Davis, rendered progressively more sensitive to slavery's worldwide unpopularity by the reports of Confederate diplomats in Europe, may have de-emphasized its centrality to the southern cause for pragmatic reasons; but Confederates addressing national, rather than international, audiences did not follow his example. Although Frank Vandiver, among others, has seen Alexander Stephens' position as the exception to the "moderate posture struck by every other Confederate" on the slave question, Davis, not Stephens, was in reality the anomaly.[2]

Leaders of the secession movement across the South cited slavery as the most compelling reason for southern independence. To Alabama convention delegate G. T. Yelverton, it was unquestionably "the cause of secession"; T. F. Goode used almost identical terms in speaking to Virginia's delegates; and Arkansas' governor told his state's convention that slavery was "now upon its trial before you." The secession conventions that drew up formal statements of the causes for their actions almost uniformly invoked the defense of slavery as their central rationalization. "Our position is thoroughly identified with the institution of slavery," the

Mississippi convention explained. Abolitionist agitation had left the South no choice but independence. Even a Confederate geography text echoed the refrain, mixing metaphors to declare slavery the "corner stone" of the nation's "governmental fabric." Journalists throughout the South reiterated and reinforced the identification of not just southern politics, but the fundamental character of the South itself with slavery. A Georgia editor put it most succinctly, observing that "negro slavery is the South, and the South is negro slavery," while Virginian George Bagby, writing as "Gamma" in the Mobile *Register,* warned that "slavery and the cause must rise or fall together, for they are identical." "Now what are we fighting for?" the *Daily Richmond Enquirer* asked as late as November, 1864. "We are fighting for the idea of race." The Augusta *Daily Constitutionalist* agreed: "Our ideal is a PRO-SLAVERY REPUBLIC." Far from marginal within Confederate nationalism, slavery was central to southerners' understanding of their purposes.[3]

As in antebellum defenses of human bondage, Confederates saw more at stake than mere political or economic self-interest. Slavery became, in both secular and religious discourse, the central component of the mission God had designed for the South. The war had "set the seal of providence before the eyes of the world upon . . . domestic slavery," noted the author of *The Historic Significance of the Southern Revolution.* "Above all, it is this that lends an awful sacredness to this contest on our part—that the rightful claims of Jehovah are deeply involved." The Confederates were fighting a just war not only because they were, in the traditional framework of just war theory, defending themselves against invasion; they were struggling to carry out God's designs for a heathen race. This was an ultimate and transcendent rationalization for both the war and southern independence. "We do not place our cause upon its highest level," Bishop Elliott explained to an 1862 fast-day congregation, "until we grasp the idea that God has made us the guardians and champions of a people whom he is preparing for his own purposes and against whom the whole world is banded." Superintending inferior, helpless Africans, assisting in their "remedial advancement," converting them to Christianity, protecting them from the destructive notions prevalent in much of the rest of the world—these were God's purposes for the South. By raising the Confederacy to national greatness, God would show the world "that it is the best form of society"—one in which he had "reconciled the long conflict of capital and labor. . . . For such a mission," an Alabama Baptist preacher asserted, "I confidently believe GOD is preparing us." This was the Confederacy's "national chart and covenant." It was for this end that southerners had been specially chosen, and it was in this all-important particular that the Confederate conception of national covenant differed most sharply from the notions of American exceptionalism out of which it had arisen. Slavery was central, a pastoral letter of Episcopal bishops concluded, to "not only our spiritual but our national life."[4]

In such a framework of reasoning, the South's ideological isolation within an increasingly antislavery world was not a stigma or a source of guilt but a badge of righteousness and a foundation for national identity and pride. When France and England surprised southerners by failing to offer the new nation diplomatic recognition, Confederate ideologues were only reinforced in their conviction of the importance of the proslavery mission. The result of the terrible struggle between North and South, the Reverend Benjamin Palmer told the South Carolina legislature, must be "to correct the error of the world as to this whole matter of domestic slavery." Slavery would thus be a source, not of southern weakness, but of moral strength. "I am looking to the poor despised slave," Bishop Elliott explained, "as the source of our security, because I firmly believe that God will not permit his purposes to be overthrown or his arrangements to be interfered with." Clergymen, politicians, and editors alike called for a new boldness in regard to slavery. As Lewis Harvie explained to the Virginia convention in November, 1861: "We are hereafter to meet this question of slavery in a totally different spirit from that which controlled us in reference to it heretofore. We must quicken our efforts henceforth in behalf of this institution. It will become necessary for us not only to protect it, but we must legislate to extend it. We are, in fact, hereafter to become slavery propagandists."[5]

The acknowledgment of the centrality of slavery to national identity stimulated a resurgence of the proslavery argument within the Confederate South. "Our people . . . have taken up the gauntlet in the proslavery discussion," one southerner observed early in 1863. In many ways, the discourse simply reiterated themes elaborated in the essays and tracts of the late antebellum years. Clergymen repeated the biblical justifications for slavery;

politicians stressed its importance to the maintenance of republican order; essayists compared wage slavery to chattel slavery and found the former wanting. When T. W. MacMahon set out to write what he described as "a brief work, containing a comprehensive and popularly written exposition of Southern political philosophy," he admitted that he could "not claim anything like pure originality for this Essay. . . . Much of its matter may have been already familiar to the reader." Nevertheless, southerners purchased this compilation of hackneyed proslavery arguments eagerly, consuming five thousand copies within a month of its first appearance in 1862.[6]

Yet even though much was the same about the wartime defense of slavery, changed circumstances made for important new departures. The creation of a southern nation opened novel channels for dissemination of proslavery ideas. Once the South began to rely entirely on its own resources for the production of new textbooks, the defense of human bondage became a part of even the elementary school curriculum. As soon as Fleming's *Revised Elementary Spelling Book* reached its consideration of "Words of Three Syllables," slavery began to appear as a regular subject for reading and orthographic exercises. *The First Reader, for Southern Schools* assured its young pupils that "God wills that some men should be slaves, and some masters." For older children, Mrs. Marinda Moore's best-selling *Geographical Reader* included a detailed proslavery history of the United States that explained how northerners had gone "mad" on the subject of abolitionism. The president of a Methodist college in Alabama composed a moral philosophy text that explicitly refuted the arguments against human bondage in widely used antebellum instructional works. Mercer University in Georgia adopted not just new texts but a new curriculum that gave a significant place to the defense of the peculiar institution. Its 1861 catalog announced that a "portion of the Senior year will be devoted to a special study of the subject of *Slavery* . . . in order that our young men may be qualified to defend the intitutions of their country." Prospective graduates were required to participate in debates about slavery under professorial supervision, so that every student might develop "a practical mastery of the argument on that question, which of all others of earthly interest, is most important to the people of the Confederate States." At every level of schooling, southerners were to be educated and socialized not just to accept but to proselytize for a slave society.

Confederate citizenship and the defense of slavery were inextricably intertwined; theirs was to be an evangelical nationalism, with slavery as an essential component of Confederate identity.[7]

The popular as well as the educational press of the Confederacy addressed the new circumstances war had brought to the venerable institution. The genre of what might be called "faithful servant" stories appeared both as fact and fiction in innumerable southern newspapers and periodicals. The Raleigh *Register*, for example, reported as truth the tale of a slave who accompanied his master to battle, watched him die, buried him, then pined to death in grief. The Mobile *Evening News* told of a bondsman who captured three Yankees on his master's plantation, and the Augusta *Weekly Constitutionalist* described groups of slaves who gathered daily to pray for the success of the Confederate cause. Other variations on this theme included stories of servants who helped hide the family silver, protect the womenfolk, and otherwise defend slavery in a variety of ways. What better legitimation than to have the supposed victims of the institution demonstrate their support? One bondsman named Harrison Berry did so quite explicitly in a widely circulated pamphlet discussion of *Slavery and Abolitionism, as Viewed by a Georgia Slave.* "A Discontented Contraband" offered a lengthy letter to the Columbus, Georgia, *Times*, testifying that "I was very foolish to leave a good home . . . to come with the cruel, lying, swindling Yankees. . . . Instead of being free, I never was so much a slave." [8]

Confederate popular literature gave fictional slave characters a significant role in responding to Lincoln's Emancipation Proclamation. A poem entitled "Philanthropy Rebuked: A True Story," portrays an ancient retainer eloquently rejecting Yankee overtures of freedom.

> Now, Massa, dis is berry fine, dese words
>   you've spoke to me,
> No doubt you mean it kindly, but ole Dinah
>   won't be free.
> I 'spect your home's a happy one—I hope it
>   may be so—
> But I'se better in de cotton field dan 'mong
>   your hills ob snow.
>
> Ole Massa's berry good to me—and though I am
>   his slave,

He treats me like I'se kin to him—and I would
    rather have
A home in Massa's cabin, and eat his black
    bread too,
Dan leave ole Massa's children and go and
    lib wid you.
. . . .
I know I shall not suffer when I'm wrinkled,
    old and blind,
For Massa's children will be good—I nussed
    em like dey'se mine,
And Missus will take care ob me—she's good
    and kind to all—
Though I'm Dinah in de cabin and she
    Missus in de hall.

A "Southern Scene from Life" described a young child reporting
to her mammy the news that Lincoln would free the slaves. In this
poem the faithful retainer is again cast in the role of a proslavery
advocate, rejecting the opportunities for freedom offered by the
war.

"Oh! mammy, have you heard the news?"
    Thus spoke a Southern child,
As in her nurse's aged face
    She upwards glanced and smiled.
. . . .
"My little Missus, stop and res,
    You's talkin' mighty fas,
Jes look up dere and tell me what
    You see in yonder glass?
You see old mammy's wrinkly face,
    As black as any coal;
And underneath her handkercher
    Whole heaps of knotty wool.
My baby's face is red and white,
    Her skin is soft an' fine,
And on her pretty little head
    De yeler ringlets shine.
My chile, who made dis difference
    'Twixt mammy and 'twixt you?
You reads de dear Lord's blessed book,

And you can tell me true.
De good Lord said it must be so,
And honey I for one,
Wid tankful heart will always say
His holy will be done.
I tanks Mass Linkum all the same,
But when I wants for free,
I'll ask the Lord of glory,
Not buckra man like he.[9]

Popular song, too, represented black characters as slavery advocates. One of the most striking developments in the arts and cultural life during the Confederacy was the growth and widespread popularity of minstrel shows. Before 1861, minstrelsy had been largely northern in origin, with only a few Yankee troupes making visits to southern cities, chiefly in the border states. Of the genre's forty-three leading midcentury performers, for example, only five were southerners. With the outbreak of war, the audience for theater in the South changed, and so, as a result, did the pattern of performances. Soldiers seeking amusement, and refugees from the countryside, created a new urban demand for entertainment, usually of a less intellectual sort than had been provided by prewar theatricals. As one critic observed, "the great unwashed" seemed after 1861 to provide a significantly larger proportion of the Confederacy's "indiscriminate and heterogeneous audiences," and their tastes ran less to Shakespeare and Marlowe than to the "Ethiopian burlesques" offered regularly in almost every southern city. During the summer of 1862, three different minstrel groups toured Mobile, Montgomery, Atlanta, Columbus, Augusta, Charleston, and Columbia. Richmond had two troupes in residence, and the *Daily Richmond Examiner* noted that "negro minstrelsy rules at the Varieties and the Hall." Troupes played in Savannah almost till the eve of Sherman's arrival, and the minstrels in Richmond declared only a few days' intermission in deference to the city's fall to the Yankees in April, 1865.[10]

But the widening public appeal of the theater was not the only reason for the shifting significance of minstrelsy in the Confederate South. Before the war, southerners had regarded these shows as politically somewhat suspect, and not without reason. During the first decade of American minstrelsy, from approximately 1843 through 1853, the performances had romanticized the plantation

Temperance Hall.

LESSEE AND MANAGER.........................JIM CLANCY
MUSICAL DIRECTOR...............................MILLER
STAGE MANAGER.................................DAN MILLER

ONE NIGHT
MORE
OF THE
COLORED
BURLESQUE MINSTRELS

Come in, Lemons ¡

By request of many citizens the

CONFEDERATE NIGHTINGALES
Will give one other entertainment at

Temperance Hall,
ON
Saturday Evening, April 15th.

PROGRAMME!
PART FIRST.

Overture...FULL BAND.
Opening Chorus......................................CONFEDS.
Song, bonny Jean...........by request............DAN MILLER.
Song, Harry Beecher.............................B. M. JAMES.
Song, We met by chance.............................CLANCY.
Song, Let them bumb.................................BONES
Song, Mary of Argyle........................JIM CLANCY.
The Ghost story...................................COMPANY.

PART SECOND.

Fancy Dance.....................................MISS LESSLIE.
Comic Song..TODD.
Grand Burlesque, Jinny Lind.................NIGHTINGALES.
Fling de High Land..................................BONES.
Burlesque Orchestra...............................COMPANY
Somebody in de house wid Dinah....................MORTON
Popular Jigg.......................................MILLER.
DAMON AND PYTHIAS, OR, THE LONG LOST BROTHERS.
The whole to conclude with a song and dance by the company.

Admission $5. Children and servants $3. Doors open at 7 o'clock, performance commence at 8 o'clock. Strict order will be kept.

"One of the most striking developments in the arts and cultural life during the Confederacy was the growth and widespread popularity of minstrel shows." Playbill. Courtesy of the Boston Athenaeum.

and its paternalism, but had at the same time often harbored an antislavery subtext. Minstrel slaves tricked and sabotaged their masters, and some shows even presented skits that portrayed such dangerous historical figures as the slave insurrectionists Gabriel and Nat Turner. Lamentations about slavery's cruel separation of black families were a standard minstrel theme. As the slavery issue became increasingly divisive in the mid and late 1850s, northern minstrel shows expunged much of this potentially unpopular content, but southerners apparently retained their suspicion of the Yankee-generated commentary on race and slavery that minstrel shows represented. Christy's Minstrels of New York, for example, confronted such local hostility that they had reason to fear for their lives when they found themselves caught in Charleston at the moment of South Carolina's secession in December, 1860.[11]

National separation dictated an end to northern dominance of minstrelsy. The troupes playing in the Confederacy were clearly identified with the South and could be trusted to present an unambiguously proslavery message to a larger and more diverse audience than that likely to study dry proslavery essays or tracts. The Mobile *Register and Advertiser* wrote approvingly in July, 1861, of a performance by a new group of "Confederate Minstrels" composed entirely of "young men of the city." "There was," the paper noted, "an entire absence of that abolition sort of songs which have been too long tolerated on the Southern Sta[g]e, where we h[o]pe never to hear 'Swanee River' or 'Nelly Gray' again."[12]

Instead, Confederate minstrelsy offered citizens of the new nation a comforting affirmation of slavery from the mouths of actors appearing in the guise of slaves. Denied such reassurances from their own servants, southern whites sought confirmation of the legitimacy, morality, and viability of the peculiar institution from the Confederate minstrel show. In one popular number, a chorus of "Lincoln's intelligent contrabands" affirmed in unison:

I'd rather work de cotton patch
And die on corn and bacon
Dan lib up Norf on good white bread
Ob abolition makin'.[13]

The adoption of "Dixie" as the emblematic Confederate song underlined the emotional centrality of these pseudoslave performances as affirmations of the Confederate national mission and

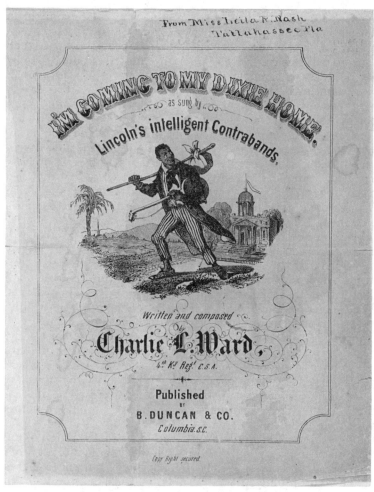

"I'd rather work de cotton patch / And die on corn and bacon / Dan lib up Norf on good white bread / Ob abolition makin'." This Confederate minstrel number portrayed slaves captured by the Union army eagerly fleeing back home to their masters. Sheet music. Courtesy of Eleanor S. Brockenbrough Library, The Museum of the Confederacy, Richmond, Virginia.

"One of the best-known Confederate renditions of this reassuring narrative of unswerving black loyalty was expressed neither in literature nor in song but in painting." *The Burial of Latané* by William D. Washington, 1864. Courtesy of the Honorable John E. DeHardit.

the master class's cherished self-image of benevolent paternalism. In the face of whatever Lincoln or the abolitionists might say about the South or its peculiar institution, "Dixie" offered the slave's unyielding desire to live and die in "de land ob cotton" as unassailable proof of the essential righteousness of the system.

One of the best-known Confederate renditions of this reassuring narrative of unswerving black loyalty was expressed neither in literature nor in song but in painting. In 1864, Virginia artist William D. Washington completed a work based upon the true story of the death of a young Confederate officer early in the war. *The Burial of Latané* depicts the makeshift funeral of one of Jeb Stuart's lieutenants, who died among strangers forbidden by surrounding enemy forces to contact either his family or a clergyman to preside at his last rites. But "the aged matron and the faithful slave" join together to inter the fallen hero and to sanctify his grave with a reading of the burial service. The artist, who lived in Richmond, undoubtedly knew of these events from a poem on the same theme, composed in 1862 by John R. Thompson, former

editor of the *Southern Literary Messenger,* and widely distributed
in broadside form. The painting proved to have even wider appeal.
Hung in a Richmond studio, it drew, one contemporary reported,
"throngs of visitors" before being moved to the state capitol.
There a bucket was placed beneath it for contributions to the
Confederate cause.[14]

The Burial of Latané was characteristic of the widely popular
genre of late eighteenth- and early nineteenth-century "grand
style" history paintings. William Washington had studied with
Emanuel Leutze and drew his inspiration from works like Benjamin West's *Death of Wolfe* and Leutze's *Washington Crossing
the Delaware.* These paintings, celebrating moments of nationalist triumph, recount politically resonant narratives that proved to
be of enormous appeal in an era of increasing popular identification with the nation-state. In their portrayal of virtue, personal
sacrifice, and heroism as the essences of national greatness, these
works invoke Christian iconography to extend a quasi-religious
dimension to their subject matter; they are visual counterparts to
the transcendent language of the era's nationalist rhetoric. Like
West's *Death of Wolfe,* Washington's *Burial of Latané* portrays a
sacrifice of human life for the larger national cause. But the painting speaks specifically to the peculiar circumstances and realities
of the Confederate situation, for it directly reflects prevailing notions of southern nationalism and the place of slavery within the
Confederacy. The ethereal light shining from the heavens and the
uplifted face of the woman serving as preacher represent the illuminating power of God's favor. The mourners assembled for
this Christian rite are a surrogate family of whites and blacks,
unknown to the deceased and to one another until cast together by
the extraordinary circumstances of war. The women are, in John
Thompson's words, "strangers, yet sisters," come like Mary to
entomb the victim of the supreme sacrifice. Yet unlike traditional
portraits of Mary receiving Christ from the cross, this southern
allusion to the hallowed artistic theme endeavors to make a statement about race, as well as about Christian suffering. Slaves lean-
ing on their shovels have obviously contributed, as always in the
South, their physical labor to make possible the ceremony wor-
shiping both God and the fallen Confederate hero.[15]

Yet the painting depicts hierarchy as well as unity. White
women and children are favored by God's light; blacks are cast
slightly into shadow. Working together, the races are still kept

carefully apart, with the slaves segregated on the left side of the painting. Physically linking them is a blond child, a representation of southern innocence and purity, who evokes, in a kind of play on symbols, the many prewar northern illustrations of Harriet Beecher Stowe's Little Eva. For Confederates gazing upon *The Burial of Latané*, the message was above all one of common Christian sacrifice in face of northern cruelty, with blacks and women uniting the homefront in support of the nation's divine mission. Representation of a ritual, the painting became itself the focal point of a new ritual of national self-affirmation for the many Confederates who thronged to see it and to add their own sacrifices to the contribution bucket below. And in *The Burial of Latané*, as in so many examples of Confederate popular literature and culture, blacks offer their consent and support to both slavery and the Confederate cause.

After more than two decades of revisionist scholarship detailing the many ways blacks struggled for their own liberation, it should hardly be necessary to point out the enormous discrepancy between the Confederate ideology of slavery and the realities of everyday life in the wartime South. Slaves were anything but consistently loyal to the peculiar institution and their masters. They fled by the thousands to Union lines and, in nearly 100,000 instances, took up arms in active combat against the Confederacy. Even slaves who remained on their plantations resisted and challenged the system of human bondage in a number of ways, such as work slowdowns and stoppages. Yet slaveowners needed to regard slavery as a benevolent institution, appreciated by blacks as well as whites, in order to preserve and propagate their self-image as paternalistic masters and to continue their own struggle for a nation-state committed to human bondage. Like the Confederate officer who was certain that his manservant had "got lost in Maryland" during the retreat from Gettysburg—until the black was captured a year later charging Confederate breastworks in Union uniform—the Confederacy as a whole clung to and even elaborated its illusions about the peculiar institution. Confederate discourse about slavery offered no acknowledgment of the disintegration of human bondage. On the contrary, the Confederate proslavery argument insisted that slaves confronted by wartime opportunities to change their status demonstrated their voluntary and enduring loyalty to their masters, to the peculiar institution, and to the Confederacy.[16]

On the one hand, such representations of slavery in the war years reaffirmed the prebellum status quo. But significantly, these treatments at the same time implicitly recognized that the conflict brought slaves the chance to exercise choices about their destiny. To cast slaves—even fictional ones—as spokesmen for the South was to empower all blacks in meaningful ways, even though this Confederate effort was designed, at least in part, to conceal or deny that war was undermining the slave system. The prominence Confederates gave to black affirmations of the peculiar institution represented a de facto loss of control by the master class. In negotiating the consensus necessary to their continuing hegemony, Confederates unwittingly imparted a legitimacy to the voices of their theoretically powerless black slaves, suggesting that their consent was somehow important to the peculiar institution's defense.

The Confederate proslavery argument made concessions to other voices as well. Confederates recognized that if slavery was to serve effectively as the cornerstone of the new nation, it must itself rest on a broader and firmer basis of support than it had previously enjoyed. Southern politicians and ideologues devoted considerable attention to the place of the nonslaveholder in southern society, recognizing the difficulties inherent in securing and retaining his support for a "proslavery republic." Throughout the 1850s, high slave prices had brought a steady decline in the percentage of white southerners owning slaves, a situation that seemed to threaten a proportionate diminution in support for the South's domestic institutions. Confederate leaders could not but fear the implications of this reality for their effort to equate the South with the slavery system and their need to call upon the southern people to make sacrifices in its behalf.

Clergymen and laymen alike addressed the troubling situation, maintaining in terms similar to those of prewar slavery advocates that the system worked very much to the benefit of the nonslaveholder. "It is upon the poorer classes of our fellow-citizens," Joseph Turner explained in the *Countryman*, "that abolition would fall in all its deadliest weight. . . . [I]t is better for the negro to serve the white man, than for one white man to serve another." Chaplain J. J. D. Renfroe delivered an empathetic proslavery oration to the men of the 10th Alabama Infantry, who were asked to risk their lives in slavery's defense. "I never owned a slave in my life, and yet I contend that I have more interest in the institution of slavery than the man who owns five hundred. Abolish the institution of slavery, and your children and my children must take the place of that institution. . . . See your posterity in cruel bondage . . . and then tell me if this is not pre-eminently the poor man's war?" The "institution of slavery," the *Southern Presbyterian Review* baldly—and wishfully—asserted, "is so interwoven . . . with the very texture of the social, political and religious life of the Southern people, that there is no diversity of interest among them." Although these questions of class became increasingly central to the proslavery arguments of the war years, southern pronouncements about the necessity of racial subordination to republican equality were hardly new. But in the Confederacy, such affirmations were often accompanied by recommendations for alterations in the place of slavery within the southern social or political order, changes that might make contentions about southern unity of interest more convincing. Although prewar apologists had called for reform to make southern society and its institutions match the ideal portrayed in their arguments, in the context of the South's bid for independence, this reformist thrust became both more possible and more necessary.[17]

Slaveowners of the Civil War South made significant concessions to the movement for *ad valorem* taxation, an attempt to increase the proportion of the tax burden borne by slave property. In Virginia, North Carolina, and Mississippi, such gestures represented an important part of the effort to broaden the consensual basis of southern rule. As one avid supporter of reform in Mississippi's laws for taxing slaves argued: "I beg leave to remind gentlemen that it is a storm *without*, against this species of property, that is the source of all our troubles, and we should be careful to give no just cause of complaint, *within*, against it. Conflicting views and opinions should be respected, and, if possible, *harmonized*." Mississippi's nonslaveholders made the logic of their appeal especially clear by tying proposed increases in slave levies to a bill for raising funds for wartime defense. If slavery had caused the war, then it should pay its fair share of the cost. Many slaveowners agreed in wartime circumstances to accept a financial burden they had resisted during the constitutional struggles of the antebellum decades. Slaves would now be taxed like other property, in proportion to their actual value rather than at an arbitrary and unrealistically low figure. By assuming this greater burden of taxation, slaveowners consciously intended to win the goodwill—and

much-needed political support of their nonslaveholding countrymen. *Ad valorem* taxation, the Richmond *Whig* promised, "will
remove every murmur of dissatisfaction throughout the confines
of the Commonwealth."[18]

In their search for national consensus, many Confederate
spokesmen recognized that their goal must be to extend slavery's
benefits, not just to lighten its burdens. At least some southerners
came to believe that the best means to such an end was to involve
more whites as slaveowners. "We must have a distribution of
slaves," an Augusta paper urged, "for many reasons, political, social, religious. For this end there ought to be, first, a law preventing any man from having more than a limited number. Say one or
two hundred." That "so small a proportion of its population is
directly interested in slavery," was, the paper warned, the South's
"heel of Achilles." In the years just prior to secession, a group of
southern extremists had inaugurated a campaign to reopen the
African slave trade. Because many southern moderates suspected
that the extremists' hidden motives were to foment discord and
disunion, the pro-slave-trade forces garnered little support.
Within the context of southern independence, however, the question assumed new relevance, for Confederate lawmakers had to
confront the issue in the drafting of new state and national constitutions. Could a nation based on slavery logically prohibit the
trade that had been the source of this honored institution? L. W.
Spratt, outspoken editor of the Charleston *Mercury*, focused on
the issue as one of the critical "tests of faith" for the new republic.
To prohibit the slave trade, he argued, was to place a stigma on the
most distinctive national trait of the Confederacy, and he insisted
on the pragmatic necessity of importing large numbers of new
slaves as the only means of establishing an enduring foundation
for the institution within the South. "Without legitimate connec-
tion with the slave," he warned, nonslaveholders "are in competi-
tion with him. They constitute *not a part of slave society*, but a
democratic society." Debate on the slave-trade issue raged
throughout the Confederacy, and a variety of concerns influenced
the ultimate prohibition of the traffic. Well before deciding on
secession, the Virginia convention considered resolving to join no
nation that permitted the trade. The Alabama convention discussed the issue at length and instructed its delegates to the national constitutional convention in Montgomery to vote against
reopening commerce. The Confederate convention finally settled

the issue by prohibiting international slave trade. In order to en-
tice border states to join the new nation the Confederacy needed
to promise them exclusive access to the profitable Deep South
market for their surplus bondsmen. But even though Spratt's solu-
tion to the narrowing of slave ownership won little support, he
articulated a widely shared recognition that the social bases of
slavery needed to be broadened if it was to serve successfully as
the defining feature of Confederate nationalism.[19]

War produced an invigorated effort to reform the internal work-
ings of the slave system as well. Throughout the antebellum
period some southerners had attempted to ameliorate slavery and
extend the bases for its ideological support by proposing laws that
placed explicit controls on masters' power. By the 1820s, for example, every southern state had passed legislation against slave
murder, and gradually a number of harsh punishments, such as
branding and mutilation, were prohibited. From the first, these
reform gestures were intended to strengthen, rather than under-
mine, the slave institution. As Eugene Genovese has noted, "The
steady progress of anti-emancipation sentiment went hand in
hand with demands for . . . greater humanity." The South was
fashioning a system of human bondage for the ages—one that its
increasingly evangelical conscience could embrace with enthusi-
asm. As proslavery tracts began multiplying in the 1830s and
1840s, the slavery reform agenda was inexorably, if ironically,
reinforced. The idyllic portrait apologists drew of the South was
more prescriptive than descriptive; their tracts implicitly recognized that "the only way to legitimate slavery was to transform
the [southern] region into the moral utopia" depicted in their essays. The call for internal changes in the slave system continued
through the 1850s, most notably in a major, though unsuccessful,
North Carolina legislative effort to recognize slave marriages and
to remove prohibitions upon slave literacy.[20]

For the Confederacy, this inherited agenda seemed to have a
newly pressing urgency. The young nation believed that it needed
to seek the widest possible support for slavery at home and abroad.
Practices that assigned slaves to permanent concubinage and prohibited them from reading the Bible were sharply dissonant with
prevailing evangelical values. "My brethren," Charles Colcock
Jones told the General Assembly of the Presbyterian Church in
1861, "the eyes of the civilized world are upon us. There are but
two other nations beside our own that hold in their bosoms the

institution of slavery. Ponder that fact and the responsibilities involved in it." If slavery were legally made the equivalent of the institution described in the Bible, another leading Presbyterian argued, it would appear "in entirely a different and milder light to the eyes of the civilized world." Southern practices were perhaps even more discordant with the Confederacy's own self-image as the missionary nation designated by God to elevate the black race to Christianity and civilization.[21]

Before the war there had been some excuse for failing to act; the North had kept the South on the defensive. "The boldest among us," Governor Zebulon Vance of North Carolina explained, "did not dare to say a word against any part of the system" because of the institution's vulnerability to abolitionist attack. But after secession, insulated by national boundaries from "Northern fanaticism," the Confederacy could feel free to act in accordance with its wishes instead of its fears; the Confederate South was obliged to work at "making slavery what it ought to be." As Calvin Wiley explained in his analysis of the causes of the South's "national trials," the "whole country being under the undisputed control of the owners of slaves, it is the duty of the governing class at once to see that justice is done to its christian sentiment and character in such civil regulations as will tend effectually to prevent a cruel or brutal master from those acts . . . which are a reflection on the dignity and justice of the state." God had waited long enough for the South to execute his designs; he would no longer tolerate violation of his trust.[22]

The chorus of voices assailing the South's neglect of religious obligations to the slaves rose steadily, first as secession gave way to full-fledged war, then as, by mid-1862, the South began to confront significant military reverses. Within the framework of Confederate self-definition, these events necessarily appeared as chastisements, warnings sent by God as calls to reformation. The Confederacy, fast-day sermons warned, had to repent of its "crying sins" by transforming slavery into a fully Christian institution. This was the inescapable logic of the proslavery argument. "God will not be mocked by us," a preacher sternly warned. "If we take His word to defend slavery, we must submit the institution to His government." The proslavery argument had developed a new corollary. Prior to the war, it had stressed that slaveholding was not sinful. But now the assertion became conditional: slavery is not sinful *if* it is practiced in obedience to God's law. Even children's textbooks echoed this new formulation. "It is not a sin to own slaves," the *Dixie Speller* assured its young readers, "but it is a very great sin to treat them cruelly." The *Geographical Reader* reiterated, "The sin of the South lies not in holding slaves, but [in that] they are sometimes mistreated."[23]

Prominent clergymen used fast-day sermons to warn legislators in Georgia, Alabama, and South Carolina of the consequences of the Confederacy's sinfulness in regard to slavery. Methodist bishop George Foster Pierce told the Georgia General Assembly that one of the "moral ends of the war is to reform the abuses of slavery" by at last placing it on a "scriptural basis." Baptist I. T. Tichenor spoke in similar terms to Alabama's governing body. "We have failed to discharge our duties to our slaves. I entertain no doubt that slavery is right, morally, socially, politically, religiously right. But there are abuses of it which ought to be corrected." God was punishing the South for neglecting its duty to the slaves, but the Confederacy still had time to repent. Independence was part of God's plan to give the South a new freedom of action in regard to slavery. But with this increased autonomy, the South assumed enhanced obligations. Only by fulfilling these duties could the Confederacy justify its new national status in God's eyes and enlist his support in its defense. Southern clergymen offered a stark equation: the new nation had been established to carry out a particular divine mission; and if it failed to do so, its struggle for existence would also fail. A committee report to the Virginia Synod in 1862 explained these contingencies clearly. "If our Southern Zion shall fully awake to the magnitude of this great work and address itself diligently to its discharge, then will she receive the rich smiles of her Divine Head, and the abundant tokens of his favor; then will the relation of master and slave, as it obtains with us, be vindicated in the eyes of the world; and then will our beloved Confederacy occupy a pinnacle of moral grandeur, and become a praise and a blessing in all the earth." The South had to fulfill its covenant with God in regard to slavery if the Confederacy was to survive.[24]

Advocates of reform agreed on which aspects of the system most needed attention and, in particular, legislative action. The barriers to Christian knowledge and conduct that were supported by state law had to be removed. Forbidding slave literacy was denying bondsmen the word of God, as well as invading the rights of the master. Prohibiting black preaching similarly separated slaves from sources of divine truth. The failure to protect slave marriages and families by law forced many southern bondsmen into illicit and unchristian conduct. Throughout the South, denominational organizations at all levels, from local congregations to nationwide conventions, appointed committees and passed resolutions on these issues. At least three state governors—Joseph Brown of Georgia, Zebulon Vance of North Carolina, and William Clark of Mississippi—expressed support for reform, and the Georgia and Mississippi legislatures made significant movement toward change. Georgia, at Brown's urging, repealed its law against slave preaching. The Georgia senate also passed a bill to repeal restriction of slave literacy, and the house judiciary committee approved protections for slave marriage; but neither measure went further before the end of the war. In 1865, the Mississippi house committee responsible for an omnibus bill on slave marriage, family relations, literacy, and murder, voted favorably on the package, but the house took no further action before the end of the war. Nevertheless, a movement was under way, with leading southern politicians and clergymen insisting on dramatic alterations of the slave institution. Had the war not ended the South's national experiment, the reform movement might well have eventually accomplished its modest goals.

It did not, of course, proceed without opposition. Some southerners feared that the timing was unpropitious, that independence had in fact increased rather than diminished the South's need to maintain a defensive posture on slavery. Reforms, they worried, would be perceived as admissions of weakness. Other opponents believed the changes would weaken the slave system by transferring control from the master to the state and the slave. As Joseph Turner, editor of the *Countryman,* explained in an attack on the slave literacy campaign, "Education and slavery are incompatible." The proposed measures, he continued, "don't strike at the root of slavery," but "they propose to lop off one of its twigs—ignorance." Even some representatives of the religious denominations most vigorously pressing reform dissented from the movement. A contributor to the *Southern Presbyterian Review* urged Christian treatment of slaves, especially in regard to their family relations, but argued that establishing slave marriage in law would be "the first and decisive step towards a total inversion of the relation of that class to the State." Slavery, the author emphasized, had always been a domestic institution in the South; the slave was subject to "family government . . . not . . . political government." To permit the slave to make contracts would be to revolutionize his status and that of the master-slave relationship upon which the whole institution rested.[25] Were the opponents of slavery reform right? Was the movement a species of covert abolitionism worming its way into the South? Certainly it was not so in intention. Its logic grew directly out of the antebellum proslavery movement. Its advocates uniformly regarded themselves as slavery's supporters and believed their actions would ensure its perpetuation. Their proposed reforms were consistent as well with the practical operation of slavery in the prewar era. The state had long intervened in the relation of master and slave. The existence of laws prohibiting whites from teaching bondsmen to read was itself an example of one such intrusion. Moreover, as much scholarly work of the past two decades has shown, slaves had, through custom, won for themselves quasi-legal rights in a number of areas of life. Many owned substantial property, contracted out their labor, limited their hours of work through the task system, or received cash payments from their masters for certain goods and services. The changes reformers requested were not inconsistent in implication with these existing arrangements.

But would the effect of reform have been to weaken slavery and set it on a course of ultimate extinction? The few twentieth-century scholars who have considered the movement believe so. Clarence Mohr, describing the fate of slavery in Georgia, sees reform leading directly to the emancipation debate that was a last gasp of the Confederate war effort. Armstead Robinson regards the movement as but one part of the larger disintegration of slavery. The "proposed reforms," he writes, "were inconsistent with the normal functioning of a slave labor based plantation economy, and indeed, most significantly, they measured the collapse of social control and concomitant death of slavery." Yet the proposed reforms were no more inconsistent with "normal functioning" than was much of the routine of slave management in the antebellum South, for the imperatives of paternalism and the establishment of absolute "social control" were inherently at odds. The conflict between the notion of absolute power and the ideology of reciprocity central to paternalism had placed contradictions at the heart of the system long before the Civil War erupted. If these inconsistencies necessarily placed slavery on the route to ultimate extinction, it had been traveling that path for a long time. And can we any longer, after comparative studies of recent decades have illuminated the great variety in forms of slavery, allude to "normal" functioning of some platonic image of "slave system"? Slavery has differed so dramatically over time and place, we must be very cautious in designating one or another attribute as "normal" or even "necessary." As David Brion Davis has observed, "The more we learn about slavery, the more difficulty we have defining it."[26]

Interpretations of Confederate slavery reform that regard change as inseparable from termination seem as well to smack of the wisdom—and narrowing of vision—inherent in hindsight, assuming Union victory and black emancipation as foregone conclusions. In other slave societies, emancipation often followed quite a different path, with some sort of interim yet enduring status of unfreedom replacing what had been called slavery. As Eric Foner has recently argued, we distort our understanding of emancipation in the United States if we regard it as bringing "*nothing* but freedom," for by doing so we underestimate the significance of that all-important achievement. The change in status for American blacks was much more dramatic than that experienced by their counterparts in other societies, where a far more gradual evolution away from legal chattel slavery took place. Caribbean islands experimented with a variety of arrangements, from apprenticeship to indentured servitude and bound labor. Without the holocaust of the Civil War, the South might have "reformed" slavery into a different sort of unfree labor, which it might well have continued to call slavery. In the 1850s, proslavery advocate Henry Hughes had argued for an updated system of slavery, which he called warranteeism. His conception called for an increase in the power of the state and a decrease in that of the master, in an institution based on "moral duty, civilly enforced." It was a notion that would have pleased Confederate reformers. Slavery would certainly have changed under these southerners' guidance, but so had it changed continually during its 250-year history in America. The ideology of Confederate reform might well have worked toward the perpetuation of southern slavery— in yet another of its ever-changing guises, but slavery nonetheless. Without the devastating pressures that war itself brought to bear upon the Confederacy and its peculiar institution, the South might have succeeded in extending slavery into the late nineteenth and perhaps even the twentieth century by legalizing some of the proposed humanistic reforms.[27] While the reforms in themselves posed little threat to the survival of the peculiar institution, the ideological configuration of slavery's wartime defense did introduce troubling elements into Confederate nationalism. Above all, the proslavery movement of the Confederacy dramatically expanded the bounds of the consent it defined as necessary to the perpetuation of the peculiar institution. Slaves were given a symbolic voice; and the burdens slavery placed on poorer whites were reduced, while the lure of slave ownership was held explicitly before them. Perhaps most significantly, southern clergy seized the initiative in Confederate public discourse about the slave system. In the prewar period, religious defenses of slavery, for all their importance to the South's self-image, seemed to follow, rather than determine, political needs. In the Confederacy, however, religion became so central to national identity and morale that clergymen felt newly empowered to take leadership roles and to define the terms of their participation in the creation of Confederate nationalism. If we are to provide you with the ideological foundations of independence, they in effect told Confederate politicians, then you must heed our prescriptions for godly behavior and moral government. If you are to use us, you must also listen to us. "God will not be mocked." You must win our consent to your rule, and the consent of God. In their zeal to rouse their countrymen to action that would still the divine chastening rod, southern clergymen seeking slavery reform resorted to the ultimate threat: "If the institution of slavery," Bishop Pierce told the Georgia assembly, "cannot be maintained except at the expense of the black man's immortal interests, in the name of Heaven I say—*let it perish.*" It seems safe to suggest that the Georgia assembly had never before listened to anything so close to an abolitionist proclamation. The centrality of religion to Confederate nationalism gave the clergy extraordinary power in shaping the South's wartime ideology.[28]

The Confederate proslavery argument, in its need to reach out for widespread moral and political consent, represented an important shift in the terms of southern hegemony—an opening of public discourse, an empowerment of new speakers and new messages, a change in the slavery system significant not so much for the particular legal reforms proposed, but for the alterations in the context of legitimation in which it rested.

V

Conclusion

Like the wartime proslavery argument, Confederate nationalism constituted a discourse about power and change. Within the framework of national identity, Civil War southerners explored the social and political meaning of independence, confronting as their forefathers had nearly a century earlier the vexing questions, not just of home rule, but of who should rule at home.

On several parallel levels, mid-nineteenth-century southern whites regarded power as part of a system of reciprocity. Within the paternalistic ethos of slavery, masters and slaves were theoretically tied by bonds of mutual obligation: the inferior to labor at the master's behest, the superior to provide sustenance and protection. White class relations were envisioned in analogous terms, with republican notions of rule by the virtuous reinforcing both the *noblesse* and the *oblige* of the master class. At the same time, the widely shared tenets of Christian evangelicalism located all the region's inhabitants in another association of reciprocity with a force superior even to the southern masters. Within the terms of the covenant theology that Confederates embraced as a central component of their emerging nationalism, southerners stood in a relationship of benefit and obligation with God, who had anointed them with both a special status and special responsibilities.

Yet developing Confederate nationalism identified imbalances in each of these dyads of mutuality. White southerners had fallen short in their duties as both servants and masters; they were fulfilling their obligations neither to God, nor to their unconverted slaves, nor to the increasing numbers of their hungry fellow countrymen. Perpetuation of the existing social order required a redress of these injustices; the demands and obligations of power necessitated change. At the same time that it promised the restoration of a lost equilibrium on which the organic unity of the South had been based, the logic of Confederate ideology prescribed an effort to build a social consensus that would have implied a significant transformation in southern life. Although southerners sought independence as a strategy for maintaining power and resisting change, the process of creating Confederate nationalism ironically and inevitably helped to create dramatic shifts in the foundations of southern society and politics.

In forging their nationalist doctrine, southerners confronted both social and intellectual constraints; they were compelled to negotiate with different social groups on the one hand, and, on the other, with the logic of the idea systems central to the process of self-legitimation. Wartime exigencies significantly empowered ordinary whites as well as black slaves in ways consistent with many of the populist, antinomian, subversively democratizing implications of evangelicalism and nationalism. For all its initially reactionary designs, for all its dedication to preserving the rights associated with its peculiar species of property, the southern elite was from the outset of the war pushed into mediating every aspect of its rule. Occasionally the paradoxical nature of its nationalist enterprise became eloquently clear, as when convention leaders sought popular votes to ratify the elimination of universal suffrage.

The ideological foundations of nationalism required popular consent; nationalism, not to mention total war, necessarily involved and thus empowered the people at large. Similarly, evangelicalism, for all its usefulness in legitimating hierarchy and control, privileged each person's relationship with God, be that individual a master, poor white, woman, or slave. The humanitarian and egalitarian components of Christianity reinforced the Confederacy's search for both popular and divine approval, just as the evangelical notion of mission made improvement, and thus change, an essential part of the Confederate agenda. By invoking religion in its support, the Confederacy necessarily embraced these imperatives as well. As southern clergymen warned, "God will not be mocked." The protean nature and paradoxical implications of both evangelicalism and republicanism thus ultimately made them deceptively weak ideological foundations. The very qualities of malleability and almost universal appeal that had transformed them into a common vocabulary of public discourse in the antebellum years rendered them less than ideal as a cement for national unity in time of war.

Confederate nationalism prescribed change in the service of continuity, but then proved able neither to contain nor explain the ensuing transformations. In the context of war, many of the dualities that had characterized the Old South emerged as inescapable social conflicts and ideological contradictions, realities with which southerners were ill-equipped to cope. The language Civil War southerners used to explicate their social world stressed concepts like harmony, reciprocity, duty, and dependence, alongside metaphors of family and of organic unity. The notion of essentially conflicting interests within a single social or political order was incompatible with Confederate thought and belief, as it was with the republican, evangelical, and nationalist doctrines on which that ideology was based. This was at once Confederate nationalism's strength and its weakness: it prescribed a necessary unity, yet could neither interpret, resolve, nor control those emergent social frictions that nationalism and national identity ironically did much to foster. The substance of Confederate nationalism, rather than the quantity or quality of its adherents' faith, was thus the ultimate source of its disintegration. Confederate ideology was defeated in large measure by the internal contradictions that wartime circumstances brought so prominently to the fore.

Yet for historians' purposes, the Confederate refraction and restatement of these issues is invaluable, for it casts into boldest relief the very assumptions on which the Old South and the Confederacy were built. Confederate nationalism was at once critique and defense of the South. As a result, it embodied perhaps the fullest discussion and definition of the issues central to that bygone civilization. The moment when southerners explained themselves to themselves was the moment they came closest to explaining themselves to us. But the nature of Confederate ideology also reminds us of the social, political, and economic constraints within which such a system of belief had necessarily to be fashioned. Ideas have a logic that derives both from themselves and their circumstances. In building Confederate nationalism, southerners fully anticipated the implications of neither. Just as the war so many southerners expected to end within a few weeks became a conflagration unlike anything mankind had known before, so too their efforts at constructing a public ideology yielded unimagined consequences. The creation of Confederate nationalism represented an apotheosis of the Old South at the same time it introduced glimmerings of the New; it caught the South within the paradoxes of that very change the Confederate nation had been founded to avert.

Notes

Chapter 1

1. E. Merton Coulter, *The Confederate State of America, 1861–1865* (Baton Rouge, 1950), 567, vol. VII of Wendell Holmes Stephenson and E. Merton Coulter (eds.), *A History of the South*. For differing interpretations of the causes of the war, see Kenneth M. Stampp (ed.), *The Causes of the Civil War* (Englewood Cliffs, 1965). See also C. Vann Woodward, *The Burden of Southern History* (Rev. ed.; New York, 1969); Charles Reagan Wilson, *Baptized in Blood: The Religion of the Lost Cause, 1865–1920* (Athens, Ga., 1980).

2. Paul M. Gaston, *The New South Creed: A Study in Southern Mythmaking* (New York, 1970); Wilson, *Baptized in Blood*; Gaines M. Foster, *Ghosts of the Confederacy: Defeat, the Lost Cause, and the Emergence of the New South* (New York, 1987).

3. See, for example, Richard N. Current, "God and the Strongest Battalions," in David Donald (ed.), *Why the North Won the Civil War* (Baton Rouge, 1960). For a useful recent overview of this historiography, see Richard E. Beringer et al., *Why the South Lost the Civil War* (Athens, Ga., 1986), Chap. I; but see also my reservations about their viewpoint, in Drew Gilpin Faust, "Reassessing the Lost Cause of the South," Philadelphia *Inquirer*, June 29, 1986, "Books/Leisure," pp. 1, 8–9.

4. See, for example, Kenneth M. Stampp, "The Southern Road to Appomattox," in Stampp, *The Imperiled Union: Essays on the Background of the Civil War* (New York, 1980); Bell Irvin Wiley, *The Road to Appomattox* (Memphis, 1956); Charles H. Wesley, *The Collapse of the Confederacy* (Washington, D.C., 1937); Frank Lawrence Owsley, "Defeatism in the Confederacy," *North Carolina Historical Review,* III (July, 1926), 446–56, and *State Rights in the Confederacy* (Chicago, 1925); Clement Eaton, "The Loss of the Will to Fight," in *A History of the Southern Confederacy* (New York, 1954); Carl N. Degler, *Place over Time: The Continuity of Southern Distinctiveness* (Baton Rouge, 1977); Charles Grier Sellers, Jr., "The Travail of Slavery," in Sellers, *The Southerner as American* (Chapel Hill, 1960).

5. Steven A. Channing, "Slavery and Confederate Nationalism," in Walter J. Fraser and Winifred B. Moore (eds.), *From the Old South to the New: Essays on the Transitional South* (Westport, Conn., 1981), 219; David M. Potter, *The South and the Sectional Conflict* (Baton Rouge, 1968), 46, 63.

6. For a comparative consideration of the Civil War and Vietnam, see James Reston, Jr., *Sherman's March and Vietnam* (New York, 1984).

7. Eugene D. Genovese, *The Political Economy of Slavery: Studies in the Economy and Society of the Slave South* (New York, 1965), *Roll, Jordan, Roll: The World the Slaves Made* (New York, 1974), and *The World the Slaveholders Made: Two Essays in Interpretation* (New York, 1969); Elizabeth Fox-Genovese and Eugene D. Genovese, *Fruits of Merchant Capital: Slavery and Bourgeois Property in the Rise and Expansion of Capitalism* (New York, 1983); Degler, *Place over Time*; Sellers, "The Travail of Slavery"; "genuine" appears in Stampp, "The Southern Road to Appomattox," 255.

8. S. A. Channing, "Slavery and Confederate Nationalism," 222–23. See also Eric Hobsbawm, "Some Reflections on Nationalism," in T. J. Nossiter, A. H. Hanson, and Stein Rokkan (eds.), *Imagination and Precision in the Social Sciences: Essays in Memory of Peter Nettl* (New York, 1972), 386.

9. The quotation is Clifford Geertz's description of Talcott Parsons' view of ideology. Geertz, "Ideology as a Cultural System," *The Interpretation of Cul-*

tures (New York, 1973), 199. See also Werner Stark, *The Sociology of Knowledge* (London, 1958), and Talcott Parsons, "An Approach to the Sociology of Knowledge," in *Transactions of the Fourth World Congress of Sociology* (Milan, 1959), 25–49. See John Higham and Paul K. Conkin (eds.), *New Directions in American Intellectual History* (Baltimore, 1979). Examples of studies in southern history that cite Geertz are: Rhys Isaac, *The Transformation of Virginia, 1740–1790* (Chapel Hill, 1982); T. H. Breen, "Horses and Gentlemen: The Cultural Significance of Gambling Among the Gentry of Virginia," in Breen, *Puritans and Adventurers: Change and Persistence in Early America* (New York, 1980); John McCardell, *The Idea of a Southern Nation: Southern Nationalists and Southern Nationalism, 1830–1860* (New York, 1979); Drew Gilpin Faust, *A Sacred Circle: The Dilemma of the Intellectual in the Old South, 1840–1860* (Baltimore, 1977, 1986). See also Ronald G. Walters, "Signs of the Times: Clifford Geertz and the Historians," *Social Research*, XLVII (Autumn, 1980), 537–56.

10. Emory M. Thomas, *The Confederate Nation, 1861–1865* (New York, 1979), 298. Many exploring southern nationalism in the Civil War use evidence almost exclusively from the antebellum period, which, I have suggested, may be their true interest in any case. Stampp, Sellers, and Degler focus on such prewar material.

11. George L. Mosse, *Nazi Culture: Intellectual, Cultural, and Social Life in the Third Reich* (New York, 1966); Tracy H. Koon, *Believe, Obey, Fight: Political Socialization of Youth in Fascist Italy, 1922–1943* (Chapel Hill, 1985); Leila Rupp, *Mobilizing Women for War: German and American Propaganda, 1939–1945* (Princeton, 1978); Victoria De Grazia, *The Culture of Consent: Mass Organization of Leisure in Fascist Italy* (Cambridge, 1981); Lynn Hunt, *Politics, Culture and Class in the French Revolution* (Berkeley, 1984), and "Engraving the Republic," *History Today*, XXX (October, 1980), 11–17; Maurice Agulhon, *Marianne into Battle: Republican Imagery and Symbolism in France, 1789–1880* (Cambridge, 1979); Mona Ozouf, *La Fête révolutionnaire* (Paris, 1976); Hugh Trevor-Roper, "The Invention of Tradition: The Highland Tradition of Scotland," and Prys Morgan, "From a Death to a View: The Hunt for the Welsh Past in the Romantic Period," in Eric Hobsbawm and Terence Ranger (eds.), *The Invention of Tradition* (New York, 1983).

12. "Insufficient" is used by Beringer *et al.*, *Why the South Lost*, 439. For influential renderings of the "spiritual" view of nationalism, see Hans Kohn, *The Idea of Nationalism: A Study of Its Origins and Background* (New York, 1944), and Carlton J. H. Hayes, *The Historical Evolution of Modern Nationalism* (New York, 1948). For a contrasting view of nationalism as process, see Hobsbawm, "Some Reflections," 394, and Geertz, "After the Revolution: The Fate of Nationalism in the New States," in *The Interpretation of Cultures*. For explorations of war as a creator of nationalism, see Charles Royster, "Founding a Nation in Blood: Military Conflict and American Nationality," in Ronald Hoffman and Peter J. Albert (eds.), *Arms and Independence: The Military Character of the American Revolution* (Charlottesville, 1984), and John M. Murrin, "War, Revolution, and Nation-Making: The American Revolution Versus the Civil War" (Research paper, Philadelphia Center for Early American Studies, 1984). Explorations of Confederate nationalism that move toward considering it as a process are: Thomas, *The Confederate Nation*, 222, 224; Lawrence Powell and Michael Wayne, "Self-Interest and the Decline of Con-

federate Nationalism," in Harry Owens and James Cooke (eds.), *The Old South in the Crucible of War* (Jackson, 1983); Armstead Louis Robinson, "Day of Jubilo: Civil War and the Demise of Slavery in the Mississippi Valley, 1861–1865" (Ph.D. dissertation, University of Rochester, 1976); and Paul D. Escott, *After Secession: Jefferson Davis and the Failure of Confederate Nationalism* (Baton Rouge, 1978).

13. On myth and southern history, see George B. Tindall, "Mythology: A New Frontier in Southern History," in Frank E. Vandiver (ed.), *The Idea of the South: Pursuit of a Central Theme* (Chicago, 1964).

14. William N. Bilbo, *The Past, Present, and Future of the Southern Confederacy: An Oration Delivered . . . October 12, 1861* (Nashville, 1861), 26; Charles W. Smythe, *Our Own Primary Grammar* (Greensborough, N.C., 1862), 1; "The True Question," *Southern Literary Messenger,* XXXIII (July, 1861), 20; *Age,* I (February, 1864), 160; *Address of the Atlanta Register to the People of the Confederate States* (Atlanta, 1864), 13; *Smith and Barrow's Monthly Magazine,* I (May, 1864), 38. See also Henry Timrod, "Southern Literature," *Daily South Carolinian,* January 16, 1864.

15. Montgomery *Daily Advertiser,* March 26, 1861; Montgomery *Daily Mail,* February 16, 1861.

16. "The Flags of the Confederacy," vol. X of United Daughters of the Confederacy Scrapbooks (Museum of the Confederacy, Richmond); Lucile Dufner, "The Flags of the Confederate States of America" (M.A. thesis, University of Texas, 1944); J. Emma Conrad to Mrs. Robert E. Lee, December 25, 1862, and March 26, 1863, both in J. Emma Conrad Papers, Museum of the Confederacy; Coulter, *The Confederate States,* 509; *Southern Monthly,* I (September, 1861), 6.

17. Robert L. Meriwether attributes articles in the *Southern Quarterly Review* on Guizot, Herder, Michelet, and Lamartine to Jamison, in *Dictionary of American Biography,* V, 604–605. See also George Frederick Holmes, "Herder's Philosophy of History," *Southern Quarterly Review,* V (April, 1844), 265–311, and "Schlegel's Philosophy of History," *Southern Quarterly Review,* III (April, 1843), 263–317; and H. Y. Riddle, "Lamartine's Travels in the East," *Southern Monthly,* I (October, 1861), 117–20. For an example of an avid reader of Lamartine, see Sarah Wadley Diary, January 14, July 27, and August 13, 1864 (Southern Historical Collection, University of North Carolina, Chapel Hill). See also Rollin G. Osterweis, *Romanticism and Nationalism in the Old South* (1949; rpr. Baton Rouge, 1971), especially Chap. X. Samuel Langhorne Clemens [Mark Twain], *Life on the Mississippi* (1883; rpr. New York, 1984), 328; Osterweis, *Romanticism and Nationalism,* Chap. IV; Grace Warren Landrum, "Sir Walter Scott and His Literary Rivals in the Old South," *American Literature,* II (November, 1930), 256–76, and "Notes on the Reading Matter of the Old South," *American Literature,* III (March, 1931), 60–71. See also Priscilla M. Bond Diary, February 11, 1864 (Manuscripts Collection, Hill Memorial Library, Louisiana State University). On the popularity of Scott among soldiers, see David Kaser, *Books and Libraries in Camp and Battle: The Civil War Experience* (Westport, 1984), 18, and Fletcher Melvin Green, "Johnny Reb Could Read," in Fletcher Melvin Green, *Democracy in the Old South and Other Essays,* ed. J. Isaac Copeland (Nashville, 1969), 185.

18. "National Characteristics: The Issue of the Day," *DeBow's Review,* XXX (January, 1861), 42–53. See also J. Quitman Moore, "Southern Civiliza-

tion: Or the Norman in America," *DeBow's Review,* XXXII (January–February, 1862), 1–19.

19. "Conflict of Northern and Southern Races," *DeBow's Review,* XXXI (October–November, 1861), 394, 391. In *Ivanhoe,* Scott contrasted "churlish Saxons" and "noble Norman knights." See Osterweis, *Romanticism and Nationalism,* 48. See also "The Difference of Race Between the Northern People and the Southern People," *Southern Literary Messenger,* XXX (June, 1860), 401–409; "Panlatinism," *Age,* I (February, 1864), 155–58; J. C. W., "The South," *Southern Monthly,* I (November, 1861), 211–13.

20. Adelaide De Vendel Chaudron, *The Third Reader* . . . (Mobile, 1864), 26; *The New Texas Reader* (Houston, 1864), v; S. A. Poindexter, *Philological Reader* (Nashville, 1861), 12; Chaudron, *The Third Reader,* 13, 26–27. See also John Neely, *The Confederate States Speller & Reader* (Augusta, 1864), 37, 38, 66. Chaudron's reader went through five editions and sold forty thousand copies during the war. Rachel Bryan Stillman, "Education in the Confederate States of America, 1861–1865," (Ph.D. dissertation, University of Illinois at Champaign-Urbana, 1972), 221. Charleston *Mercury* quoted in Chaudron, *The First Reader* (Mobile, 1864), 59. On language and nationalism in France, see Eugen Weber, *Peasants into Frenchmen: The Modernization of Rural France, 1870–1914* (Stanford, 1976); and on the French Revolution specifically, see Hunt, *Politics, Culture and Class,* 83. Southerners' conceptions of the peculiarities of their own language in the mid-nineteenth century differ sharply with Cleanth Brooks's explanation of southern dialect as a perpetuation of old English pronunciations adopted by blacks as well as whites. See Brooks, *The Language of the American South* (Athens, Ga., 1985), Chap. I. On language of power, see Benedict Anderson, *Imagined Communities: Reflections on the Origin and Spread of Nationalism* (London, 1983), 48.

21. For examples of versions of the "Marseillaise," see "Southern Marseillaise," in *Songs of the South* (Richmond, 1863), 34, and in *The Bonnie Blue Flag Song Book* (Augusta, 1863), 25; Huntsville (Ala.) *Democrat,* January 3, 1861; "Texas Marseillaise," in H. M. Wharton (ed.), *War Songs and Poems of the Southern Confederacy, 1861–1865* (Philadelphia, 1904), 191; "The Power of Song," clipping from Richmond *Whig* in Mary Dickinson Scrapbook (Manuscripts Collection, Hill Memorial Library, Louisiana State University); and a playbill advertising "The Concert! Saturday September 28, 1861" (Austin, 1861). "Tocsin" quote from the May 31 entry in Unknown Woman's Diary, 1864 (Virginia State Library, Richmond); Richard Barksdale Harwell, *Confederate Music* (Chapel Hill, 1950), and *Songs of the Confederacy* (New York, 1951), 29.

22. *Daily Richmond Enquirer,* November 13, 1861; "Panlatinism," 158; "The Rise of Nations: The New Italian Kingdom and the Southern Confederacy," *Weekly Spy* (Covington, Tenn.), March 30, 1861; "European Correspondence," Charleston *Daily Courier,* April 16, 1861; "Patriotism," *Southern Monthly,* I (September, 1861), 6; "Motley's Dutch Republic," *Southern Presbyterian Review,* XV (July, 1862), 148; "Poland," *Daily Richmond Enquirer,* March 16, 1863. On Poland, see also Montgomery *Daily Advertiser,* April 1, 1861; Mobile *Evening News,* August 8, 1864; "The Insurrection of Poland," *The Record of News, History and Literature,* I (September 3, 1863), 106. On the South's earlier reaction to Louis Kossuth as too liberal an embodiment of

nationalism, see Donald S. Spencer, *Louis Kossuth and Young America: A Study of Sectionalism and Foreign Policy, 1848–1852* (Columbia, Mo., 1977). See also Charles M. Wiltse, "A Critical Southerner: John C. Calhoun on the Revolution of 1848," *Journal of Southern History*, XV (August, 1949), 299–310.
23. Robert Toombs, "Inclosure, Memorandum of Instructions for Mr. John T. Pickett, May 17, 1861," in James D. Richardson (ed.), *The Messages and Papers of Jefferson Davis and the Confederacy, Including Diplomatic Correspondence, 1861–1865* (New York, 1966), II, 25, 24.
24. See, for example, Jefferson Davis, "Inaugural Address," in Richardson (ed.), *The Messages and Papers of the Confederacy*, I, 32–36.
25. "Southern Warcry," in *Hopkins' New-Orleans 5 Cent Song-book* (New Orleans, 1861), 7; "Jefferson Davis," in *The Southern Soldier's Prize Songster* (Mobile, 1864), 80; "God Save the South," in *The Army Songster* (Richmond, 1864), 64–65. See also "Seventy-Six and Sixty One," in *The Southern Soldier's Prize Songster*, 13.
26. William Gilmore Simms, *The History of South Carolina from Its Erection into a Republic; With a Supplementary Book, Bringing the Narrative Down to the Present Time* (New York, 1860); McCardell, *The Idea of a Southern Nation* (New York, 1979), Massimo d'Azeglio quoted in E. J. Hobsbawm, *The Age of Capital, 1848–1875* (New York, 1975), 89.
27. T. J. Jackson Lears, "The Concept of Cultural Hegemony: Problems and Possibilities," *American Historical Review*, XC (June, 1985), 561–93.
28. Bilbo, *The Past, Present, and Future*, 26. Lynn Hunt's studies of revolutionary France have revealed a much greater popular influence upon nationalist symbolism and ideology than I have discovered in the Confederate South. There are no evident southern equivalents of such popular French symbols as the liberty tree, for example. Hunt, *Politics, Culture and Class*.
29. Anderson, *Imagined Communities*, 31. See also Karl W. Deutsch, *Nationalism and Social Communication: An Inquiry into the Foundations of Nationality* (Cambridge, Mass., 1953).
30. "Editor's Table," *Southern Literary Messenger*, XXXVIII (May, 1864), 315. On the lower levels of literacy in the South in comparison to the North, see Lee Soltow and Edward Stevens, *The Rise of Literacy and the Common School in the United States: A Socioeconomic Analysis to 1870* (Chicago, 1981).
31. *Southern Monthly*, I (December, 1861), 307; "The Existing Crisis," *DeBow's Review*, XXXII (January–February, 1862), 109; Ellen Gay Detlefson, "Printing in the Confederacy, 1861–1865: A Southern Industry in Wartime" (D.L.S. dissertation, Columbia University, 1975); Lawrence F. London, "Confederate Literature and Its Publishers," in J. Carlyle Sitterson (ed.), *Studies in Southern History in Memory of Albert Ray Newsome* (Chapel Hill, 1957), 82–96; Rabun Lee Brantley, *Georgia Journalism of the Civil War Period* (Nashville, 1929). On calls by newspapers for needed rags, see, for example, *Edgefield* (S.C.) *Advertiser*, January 21, 1863; *Daily Southern Guardian* (Columbia, S.C.), April 27, 1863. On problems of *Daily Sun* (Columbus, Ga.) procuring ink, type, and other essentials, see Thomas Gilbert & Co. Books (MSS in Southern Historical Collection). For other contemporary descriptions of publishing difficulties, see "Publishing in the Confederacy," *Daily Richmond Enquirer*, February 24, 1863; Milledgeville (Ga.) *Confederate Union*,

January 12, 1864. On the school text, see Richard Sterling, *Our Own Third Reader* (Greensboro, N.C. 1863). On the seal, see Coulter, *The Confederate States*, 119–20, and *The Record of News, History and Literature*, I (June 18, 1863), 1–2; August Dietz, *The Postal Service of the Confederate States of America* (Richmond, 1929); "Postal Policy of the Confederate States," Montgomery *Daily Advertiser*, March 15, 1861; Kenneth Millikan Brim, "The Postal Issues of the Confederate States of America, 1861–1864" (Annotated stamp album in Manuscript Division, William R. Perkins Library, Duke University). On the situation at the Richmond post office, see "Mercury" [George Bagby], Memphis *Appeal*, June 7, 1864, Scrapbook, Section 25 (George Bagby Papers, Virginia Historical Society, Richmond).

32. Coulter, *The Confederate States*, 493. See also J. Cutler Andrews, *The South Reports the Civil War* (Princeton, 1970); Bell I. Wiley, "The Camp Newspapers of the Confederacy," *North Carolina Historical Review*, XX (1943), 327–35; Edward Budget, Camp Manning Newspaper (MS in Virginia State Library); "Grape Shot," Co. A, 21 Mississippi Volunteers (MS in Museum of the Confederacy, Richmond); James W. Silver, "Propaganda in the Confederacy," *Journal of Southern History*, XI (November, 1945), 487–503.

33. Anderson, *Imagined Communities*, 132; Harwell makes a similar point, in *Confederate Music*, 5. Similarly, "group readings" of scarce Confederate newspapers also occurred; but these situations lacked the cohesiveness encouraged by group singing, for all except the reader were listeners rather than active participants. On Confederate music, see also Willard A. Heaps and Porter W. Heaps, *The Singing Sixties: The Spirit of Civil War Days Drawn from the Music of the Times* (Norman, 1960); Francis A. Lord and Arthur Wise, *Bands and Drummer Boys of the Civil War* (New York, 1979); "The Poems and Songs of the Confederacy," vol. LV of United Daughters of the Confederacy Scrapbooks (MS, Museum of the Confederacy, Richmond).

34. Jan Vansina, *Oral Tradition as History* (Madison, 1985); Harwell, *Songs of the Confederacy*, 54.

35. *Daily Richmond Enquirer*, May 21, 1862; Carlton McCarthy, *Detailed Minutiae of Soldier Life in the Army of Northern Virginia, 1861–1865* (Richmond, 1882), 106–107; "Exempt Me from the War," Columbus (Ga.) *Daily Times*, January 30, 1865; Charles C. Sawyer and Henry Tucker, *Call Me Not Back from the Echoless Shore* (Macon, n.d.).

36. See, for example, Elizabeth Sloman, *Sumter: A Ballad of 1861* (Charleston, S.C., 1861); "Battle of Bethel," in *Songs of the South* (Richmond, 1863), 14; "Stonewall Jackson," in Thomas A. Branson (comp.), *The Jack Morgan Songster* (Raleigh, 1864), 29; *The Stonewall Song Book* (Richmond, 1864); Adolphus Brown, *Genl. Joseph E. Johnston Manassas Quick March* (New Orleans, 1861); Mrs. V. G. Cowdin, *Gen. Beauregard's Grand March* (New Orleans, 1861); Miss Victoria C., *The Beauregard, or Fort Sumter Polka March* (New Orleans, 1861); C. D. Benson, *Gen. A. Sidney Johnson's Grand March* (Nashville, 1861); P. Rivinac, *Gen. Bragg Grand March* (New Orleans, 1861); Charles Young, *Gen. Lee's Quick March* (Augusta, 1863); John Prosinger, *Pickets [sic] Charge March* (Columbia, S.C., n.d.); Charles L. Ward, *Gen. Breckenridge's Grand Waltz* (Nashville, 1862); H. N. Hempstead, *Mason & Slidell Quickstep* (Nashville, 1861). Note that the enthusiastic admirers penning these songs did not even always know how to spell the names of the new heroes they were honoring.

Chapter 2

1. *Religious Herald*, January 1, 1863. See also *Daily Richmond Enquirer*, July 1, 1863, on the Confederacy being "more religiously disposed" than the Union. *Southern Christian Advocate*, April 2, 1863; clergyman quoted in James W. Silver, *Confederate Morale and Church Propaganda* (Tuscaloosa, 1957), 58; Alexander Gregg, *Primary Charge, to the Clergy of the Protestant Episcopal Church*... (Austin, 1863), 4. See also Charles W. Dabney to Robert L. Dabney, March 13, 1861, in Charles W. Dabney Papers, Southern Historical Collection, University of North Carolina, Chapel Hill. On the role of religion in the Confederacy, see also Charles Reagan Wilson, *Baptized in Blood: The Religion of the Lost Cause, 1865–1920* (Athens, Ga., 1980); William A. Clebsch, *Christian Interpretations of the Civil War* (Philadelphia, 1969); Terrie Dopp Aamodt, "Righteous Armies, Holy Cause: Apocalyptic Imagery and the Civil War" (Ph.D. dissertation, Boston University, 1986).

2. On Sumter as a divine providence, see, for example: Charleston (S.C.) *Daily Courier*, May 7, 1861; Thomas Smyth, *The Battle of Fort Sumter: Its Mystery and Miracle*... (Columbia, S.C., 1861), 8; J. H. Elliott, *The Bloodless Victory: A Sermon* ... (Charleston, S.C., 1861); Charles Colcock Jones to Charles Colcock Jones, Jr., April 20, 1861, in Robert Manson Myers (ed.), *The Children of Pride: A True Story of Georgia and the Civil War* (New Haven, 1972), 666. For an overview of just war thinking, see James Turner Johnson, *Just War Tradition and the Restraint of War: A Moral and Historical Inquiry* (Princeton, 1981). For a compelling account of war as a moral dilemma through history, see Michael Walzer, *Just and Unjust Wars: A Moral Argument with Historical Illustrations* (New York, 1977).

3. Theophilus Perry quoted in Randolph B. Campbell, *A Southern Community in Crisis: Harrison County, Texas, 1850–1880* (Austin, 1983), 239; Edwin Theodore Winkler, *Duties of the Citizen Soldier: A Sermon* ... (Charleston, S.C., 1861), 1, 7–8; Stephen Elliott, *The Silver Trumpets of the Sanctuary: A Sermon* ... (Savannah, 1861), 6–7; "Hurrah, My Brave Boys," in *Songs of the South* (Richmond, 1862), 19; Earnest Halphin and Chas. W. A. Ellerbrock, *God Save the South!* (Augusta, 1861); Rev. Wm. F. Broaddus, *In Camp* (N.p., n.d.), 3.

4. *Biblical Recorder*, July 17, 1861; Joseph H. Echols, *Speech of . . . Jan. 19, 1865* (Richmond, 1865), 1.

5. *The Record of News, History and Literature*, I (June 18, 1863), 1–2; Richmond *Christian Observer*, January 23, 1862; Stephen Elliott, *Ezra's Dilemna* [sic]: *A Sermon* ... (Savannah, 1863), 17.

6. Nathan O. Hatch, *The Sacred Cause of Liberty: Republican Thought and the Millennium in Revolutionary New England* (New Haven, 1977), 3; Rev. W. H. Ruffner, *The Oath: A Sermon* ... (Lexington, Va., 1864), 11. See also James H. Moorhead, *American Apocalypse: Yankee Protestants and the Civil War, 1860–1869* (New Haven, 1978).

7. Perry Miller, *Errand into the Wilderness* (Cambridge, 1958), *The New England Mind: From Colony to Province* (Cambridge, 1953); Sacvan Bercovitch, *The American Jeremiad* (Madison, 1978). For discussion of a pre–Civil War invocation of the jeremiad in the South, see Drew Gilpin Faust, "The Rhetoric and Ritual of Agriculture in Antebellum South Carolina," *Journal of Southern History*, XLV (November, 1979), 541–68. See also Mitchell Snay, "Gospel of Disunion: Religion and the Rise of Southern Separatism,

1830–1861" (Ph.D. dissertation, Brandeis University, 1984). Rev. E. H. Harding explicitly saw himself as a latter-day Jeremiah preaching to the South. See Harding to My Dear Mary, June 10, 1862, in Historical Foundation of the Presbyterian Church, Montreat, N.C.; Alexander Sinclair, A Thanksgiving Sermon, Preached in the Presbyterian Church at Six-Mile Creek, Lancaster District, S.C. . . . (N.p., 1862), 14; Our Triumph. By the Author of "The Countersign" (Richmond, 1864), 1. On Puritans, see also "A Religious People," Augusta Weekly Constitutionalist, August 6, 1862, which addresses the tradition of the fast day; and "The Puritans," Southern Presbyterian Review, XV (October, 1862), 230–55. On fast day tradition, see William Gribben, The Churches Militant: The War of 1812 and American Religion (New Haven, 1973), and Emory Elliott, Power and the Pulpit in Puritan New England (Princeton, 1975). On religious conceptions of American destiny, see: Ernest Lee Tuveson, Redeemer Nation: The Idea of America's Millennial Role (Chicago, 1968); Conrad Cherry, God's New Israel: Religious Interpretations of American Destiny (Englewood Cliffs, 1971); and Paul C. Nagel, This Sacred Trust: American Nationality, 1798–1898 (New York, 1971).

8. Stephen Elliott, Gideon's Water-Lappers: A Sermon . . . (Macon, 1864), 20; B. M. Palmer, National Responsibility Before God: A Discourse, Delivered on the Day of Fasting, Humiliation and Prayer . . . (New Orleans, 1861), 9, 6–7; J. Henry Smith, A Sermon Delivered at Greensboro, N.C. . . . (Greensboro, N.C., 1862), 11. On Elliott, see William A. Clebsch, "Stephen Elliott's View of the Civil War," Historical Magazine of the Protestant Episcopal Church, XXXI (March, 1962), 7–20; Dwyn Mouger, "History as Interpreted by Stephen Elliott," Historical Magazine of the Protestant Episcopal Church, XLIV (September, 1975), 285–318; and Edgar L. Pennington, "Bishop Stephen Elliott and the Confederate Episcopal Church," Georgia Review, IV (April, 1950), 233–47.

9. On God as a nationalist, see J. L. Burrows, Nationality Insured: Notes of a Sermon . . . (Augusta, 1864).

10. J. P. Philpott, The Kingdom of Israel . . . (Fairfield, Tex., 1864), 45; J. Jones, The Southern Soldier's Duty: A Discourse . . . (Rome, Ga., 1861); William C. Butler, Sermon: Preached in St. John's Church, Richmond . . . (Richmond, 1861), 5. See also Confederate Baptist, November 26, 1862; Religious Herald, November 6, 1862; W. H. Seat, The Confederate States of America in Prophecy (Nashville, 1861); Daniel I. Dreher, A Sermon . . . (Salisbury, N.C., 1861); T. S. Winn, The Great Victory at Manassas' Junction . . . (Tuskaloosa [sic], Ala., 1861).

11. Montgomery Daily Advertiser, September 8, 1862; O. S. Barten, A Sermon Preached in St. James' Church, Warrenton, Va. . . . (Richmond, 1861), 7. See also Palmer, National Responsibility; "The Law of the Sabbath and Its Bearing upon National Prosperity," Southern Presbyterian Review, XV (July, 1862), 30.

12. Southern Christian Advocate, March 26, 1863. See also Minutes of the Evangelical Lutheran Synod of South Carolina (Columbia, S.C., 1862), 5; Religious Herald, March 13, 1862; Henry Holcombe Tucker, God in the War: A Sermon . . . (Milledgeville, Ga., 1861), 16. On the nature of reform in the Old South, see Drew Gilpin Faust, A Sacred Circle: The Dilemma of the Intellectual in the Old South, 1840–1860 (Baltimore, 1977), 80–86; James H. Moorhead, "Social Reform and the Divided Conscience of Antebellum Protestantism," Church History, XLVIII (December, 1979), 416–30.

13. Stephen Elliott, *"New Wine Not to Be Put into Old Bottles": A Sermon* . . . (Savannah, 1862), 9; Mobile *Evening News*, January 11, 1864. For examples of ready acceptance of such fast-day sermon sentiments, see Priscilla M. Bond Diary, February 2 and March 6, 1864, and Mary A. Dickinson Scrapbook, November 13 and 15, 1861 (Manuscripts Collection, Hill Memorial Library, Louisiana State University, Baton Rouge).

14. Palmer, *National Responsibility*, 18. The literature on republicanism has become too voluminous to cite here. Particularly useful in this context, however, are Drew R. McCoy, *The Elusive Republic: Political Economy in Jeffersonian America* (Chapel Hill, 1980), and James Oakes, "From Republicanism to Liberalism: Ideological Change and the Crisis of the Old South," *American Quarterly*, XXXVII (Fall, 1985), 551–71.

15. Marinda Branson Moore, *The Geographical Reader, for the Dixie Children* (Raleigh, 1863), 39; "The Law of the Sabbath," 23. See also resolutions to repeal Sabbath mails, "The General Assembly of Columbia," *Southern Presbyterian Review*, XVI (July, 1863), 102. Later in the war, some northern clergymen pushed for a similar revision of the U.S. Constitution. Moorhead, *American Apocalypse*, 141; Myers (ed.), *The Children of Pride*, 725; "Dr. Thornwell's Memorial on the Recognition of Christianity in the Constitution," *Southern Presbyterian Review*, XVI (July, 1863), 81. See also James Oscar Farmer, Jr., *The Metaphysical Confederacy: James Henley Thornwell and the Synthesis of Southern Values* (Macon, 1986).

16. Calvin H. Wiley, *Scriptural Views of National Trials: Or the True Road to the Independence and Peace of the Confederate States of America* (Greensboro, N.C., 1863), 172; George F. Pierce and B. M. Palmer, *Sermons . . . Delivered Before the General Assembly at Milledgeville, Ga. . . .* (Milledgeville, 1863), 9. See also Palmer, *National Responsibility*, 19; Alexander Gregg, *Primary Charge*, 16. For a discussion of the reactionary potential within southern republicanism, see Drew Gilpin Faust, *James Henry Hammond and the Old South: A Design for Mastery* (Baton Rouge, 1982), 40–43.

17. See Farmer, *The Metaphysical Confederacy*, 189–90; Jack P. Maddex, "From Theocracy to Spirituality: The Southern Presbyterian Reversal in Church and State," *Journal of Presbyterian History*, LIV (Winter, 1976), 438–57; Alexander Gregg, *Primary Charge*, 4; Richmond *Christian Observer*, August 14, 1862; Ernest Trice Thompson, *Presbyterians in the South, 1861–1890* (Richmond, 1973), II.

18. Stephen Elliott, *How to Renew Our National Strength: A Sermon* . . . (Richmond, 1862), 9; J. C. Stiles, *National Rectitude the Only True Basis of National Prosperity: An Appeal to the Confederate States* (Petersburg, Va., 1863), 32. See also *Daily Richmond Enquirer*, February 6, 1861, and William Norwood, *God and Our Country: A Sermon . . .* (Richmond, 1863); Analytica [pseud.], *The Problem of Government, in the Light of the Past, Present and the Future* (Richmond, 1862), 22–23. Davis quoted in Sylvanus Landrum, *The Battle Is God's: A Discourse . . .* (Savannah, 1863), 3.

19. *Confederate Baptist*, March 4, 1863. See also "Is It a Sin to Differ with the Administration?" Augusta *Daily Constitutionalist*, May 3, 1864, and J. J. D. Renfroe, *"The Battle Is God's": A Sermon . . .* (Richmond, 1863).

20. *Daily Richmond Enquirer*, April 28, 1863; Fletcher M. Green, *Constitutional Development in the South Atlantic States, 1776–1860: A Study in the Evolution of Democracy* (Chapel Hill, 1930).

21. Allen D. Candler (comp.), *The Confederate Records of the State of Georgia* (Atlanta, 1909), II, 369.

22. J. S. Clarke quoted in *Journal of the Convention of the People of the State of Alabama* (Montgomery, 1861), 198–99; William R. Smith, *The History and Debates of the Convention of the People of Alabama* (Montgomery, 1861), 267. For one of the Charleston (S.C.) *Daily Courier*'s many attacks on the South Carolina convention, see "The Convention and the Executive Council," July 16, 1862. An influential study that focuses almost exclusively on the secession actions of the conventions is Ralph A. Wooster, *The Secession Conventions of the South* (Princeton, 1962). The Alabama convention debated its powers at considerable length. See Smith, *The History . . . of the Convention . . . of Alabama*, 277–92; *Journal of the Convention . . . of Alabama*. On Virginia, see *Journal of the Acts and Proceedings of a General Convention of the State of Virginia* (Richmond, 1861). Invaluable is Henry T. Shanks, "Conservative Constitutional Tendencies of the Virginia Secession Convention," in Fletcher Melvin Green (ed.), *Essays in Southern History, Presented to Joseph G. R. Hamilton* (Chapel Hill, 1949), 28–48. See also Julian A. C. Chandler, *The History of Suffrage in Virginia* (Baltimore, 1901); James Clyde McGregor, *The Disruption of Virginia* (New York, 1922); Charles Henry Ambler, *Sectionalism in Virginia from 1776 to 1861* (Chicago, 1910); Henry T. Shanks, *The Secession Movement in Virginia* (Richmond, 1934); Robert H. Turner, "Recollections of the Virginia Convention of 1861" (MS in Virginia Historical Society). See also Saunders Family Papers, Marshall Family Papers, Robert Y. Conrad Papers, Grinnan Family Papers, and Richard Eppes Diary, all in Virginia Historical Society. On Arkansas, see Michael B. Dougan, *Confederate Arkansas: The People and Policies of a Frontier State in Wartime* (University, Ala., 1976). On North Carolina, see J. Carlyle Sitterson, *The Secession Movement in North Carolina* (Chapel Hill, 1939); Marc W. Kruman, *Parties and Politics in North Carolina, 1836–1865* (Baton Rouge, 1983); Kent Plummer Battle, *Legislation of the Convention of 1861* (Chapel Hill, 1900); Samuel A. Ashe, *History of North Carolina* (2 vols.; Raleigh, 1925), II; *Journal of the Convention of the People of North Carolina* (Raleigh, 1862); *Ordinances and Resolutions Passed by the State Convention* (Raleigh, 1861). On South Carolina, see Charles W. Cauthen, *South Carolina Goes to War, 1860–1865* (Chapel Hill, 1950); John Amasa May and Joan Reynolds Faunt, *South Carolina Secedes* (Columbia, 1960); John B. Edmunds, *Francis W. Pickens and the Politics of Destruction* (Chapel Hill, 1986); Laura A. White, "The Fate of Calhoun's Sovereign Convention in South Carolina," *American Historical Review*, XXXIV (July, 1929), 757–71; *Journal of the Convention of the People of South Carolina, Held in 1860–'61* (Charleston, 1861); *Journal of the Convention of the People of South Carolina, Held in 1860, 1861 and 1862* (Columbia, 1862). On Georgia, see Michael P. Johnson, *Toward a Patriarchal Republic: The Secession of Georgia* (Baton Rouge, 1977); Albert Berry Saye, *A Constitutional History of Georgia, 1732–1945* (Athens, 1948); *Journal of the Public and Secret Proceedings of the Convention of the People of Georgia* (Milledgeville, 1861).

23. Smith, *The History . . . of the Convention of . . . Alabama*, 223–24; *Journal of the Convention of the People of Florida* (Tallahassee, 1862), 92. For Virginia debates on the issue, see "Proceedings of the Secession Convention," *Daily Richmond Enquirer*, March 20 and November 29, 1861; *Journal . . . of a*

General Convention of the State of Virginia, 338. For North Carolina, see *Journal of the Convention . . . of North Carolina*, 2nd session, 25. For examples of newspapers supporting citizenship restriction, see Charleston (S.C.) *Daily Courier*, August 16, 1861; Augusta *Weekly Constitutionalist*, August 14, 1861; Edgefield (S.C.) *Advertiser*, March 25, 1863. On Confederate citizenship, see also Charles Robert Lee, Jr., *The Confederate Constitutions* (Chapel Hill, 1963); James H. Kettner, *The Development of American Citizenship, 1608–1870* (Chapel Hill, 1978), 336; William M. Robinson, Jr., *Justice in Grey: A History of the Judicial System of the Confederate States of America* (Cambridge, Mass., 1941), 178–81.

24. M. P. Johnson, *Toward a Patriarchal Republic*, 143; Ruffin quoted in Shanks, "Conservative Constitutional Tendencies," 30n; *Journal of the Convention . . . of Alabama*, 178; Dougan, *Confederate Arkansas*, 63.

25. "Proceedings of Secession Convention," *Daily Richmond Enquirer*, November 20, 1861.

26. Richmond *Daily Whig*, August 21, 1861; Staunton newspaper quotation from Shanks, "Conservative Constitutional Tendencies," 43; Richmond *Daily Dispatch*, March 14, 1862; New Orleans *Crescent*, November 20, 1861.

27. New Orleans *Crescent*, November 25, 1861.

28. John Potter, in Wm. R. Smith, *The History . . . of the Convention of . . . Alabama*, 108.

Chapter 3

1. James Henley Thornwell, *Our Danger and Our Duty* (Charleston, S.C., n.d.), 12.

2. William Norwood, *God and Our Country: A Sermon . . .* (Richmond, 1863), 6; Thomas Verner Moore, *God Our Refuge and Strength in This War: A Discourse . . .* (Richmond, 1861), 7; Charles Cotesworth Pinckney, *Nebuchadnezzars's* [sic] *Fault and Fall: A Sermon . . .* (Charleston, S.C., 1861), 10; Thomas Atkinson, *Christian Duty in the Present Time of Trouble: A Sermon . . .* (Wilmington, N.C., 1861), 7; *Proceedings of the Bible Convention of the Confederate States of America . . . and Also a Sermon . . . by the Rev. George F. Pierce, D.D. . . .* (Augusta, 1862), 17; John H. Rice, *A System of Modern Geography . . . Expressly for the Use of Schools and Academies in the Confederate States of America* (Atlanta, 1862), 51; An Alabamian, "Yankee-Doodle-Doo," in *The Southern Soldier's Prize Songster* (Mobile, 1864), 19.

3. On concerns about materialism in the prewar South, see Kenneth Moore Startup, "Strangers in the Land: The Southern Clergy and the Economic Mind of the Old South" (Ph.D. dissertation, Louisiana State University, 1983).

4. On the roles of slavery and the market in the antebellum South, see Elizabeth Fox-Genovese and Eugene Genovese, *Fruits of Merchant Capital: Slavery and Bourgeois Property in the Rise and Expansion of Capitalism* (New York, 1983), and Steven Hahn, *The Roots of Southern Populism: Yeoman Farmers and the Transformation of the Georgia Upcountry, 1850–1890* (New York, 1983); James Oakes, "The Politics of Economic Development in the Antebellum South," *Journal of Interdisciplinary History*, XV (Autumn, 1984), 305–16. Also helpful on these issues are: Florencia Mallon, *The Defense of Community in Peru's Central Highlands: Peasant Struggle and Capitalist Transition, 1860–1940* (Princeton, 1983); Karl Polanyi, *The Great Transfor-*

mation (New York, 1944); Michael Merrill, "Cash Is Good to Eat: Self-Sufficiency and Exchange in the Rural Economy of the United States," *Radical History Review,* III (Winter, 1977), 42–66; and James Henretta, "Families and Farms: *Mentalité* in Pre-Industrial America," *William and Mary Quarterly,* XXXV (January, 1978), 3–32. On development in Georgia, see T. Conn Bryan, *Confederate Georgia* (Athens, Ga., 1953), 48. On South Carolina, see Lacy K. Ford, Jr., "Social Origins of a New South Carolina: The Upcountry in the Nineteenth Century" (Ph.D. dissertation, University of South Carolina, 1983), especially Chap. V.

5. T. V. Moore, *God Our Refuge and Strength in This War,* 7; George Foster Pierce, *The Word of God a Nation's Life: A Sermon* . . . (Augusta, 1862), 17; *Central Presbyterian,* July 6, 1861. For a similar belief that war would bring a welcome reversal of growing materialism, see Eric J. Leed, *No Man's Land: Combat & Identity in World War I* (New York, 1979), 46.

6. Montgomery *Daily Advertiser,* December 5, 1863.

7. George Anderson Mercer Diary, September 14, 1863 (MS in Southern Historical Collection, University of North Carolina, Chapel Hill); Alexander Gregg, *A Sermon: Preached in St. David's Church* . . . (Austin, 1863), 1; *Minutes of the Georgia Baptist Association* . . . (Macon, 1862), 5.

8. *Central Presbyterian,* April 9, 1863; Gregg, *A Sermon: Preached in St. David's Church,* 5. See also Richard Fox, Fast-day Sermon, March 7, 1865 (MS in Virginia Historical Society, Richmond).

9. *A Bill to Be Entitled an Act to Prevent Speculation, Hoarding and Extortion. Senate Bill No. 154* (Richmond, 1864); Davis quoted in Document I, *Journal of the House of Delegates of the State of Virginia, for the Adjourned Session, 1863* (Richmond, 1863), xxv; "Testimony Before the Committee on Extortion, 1863," in *Documents. Called Session, 1862, and Adjourned Session, 1863.* (Richmond, 1863), Document 22; *Journal of the Senate of the Commonwealth of Virginia . . . the Seventh Day of September, [1863] . . . Extra Session.* (Richmond, 1863), 30; *Journal of the Senate of the Commonwealth of Virginia: Begun . . . the Seventh of December, [1863]* . . . (Richmond, 1863), 59; *Journal of the House of Delegates of the State of Virginia, for the Called Session of 1862* (Richmond, 1862), 12, 14, 16, 21, 28, 33, 39, 51, 58, 60; *Journal of the House of Delegates of the State of Virginia, for the Adjourned Session, 1863* (Richmond, 1863), 81–98, and Document 1. See also *Daily Richmond Enquirer,* January 28, February 6 and 14, and October 10, 13, 20, 21, and 23, 1863; E. Merton Coulter, *The Confederate States of America, 1861–1865* (Baton Rouge, 1950), 234, vol. VII in Wendell Holmes Stephenson and E. Merton Coulter (eds.), *A History of the South. Laws of the State of Mississippi, Passed . . . November & December 1861, and January, 1862* (Jackson, 1862), 144; *Acts of the Called Session, 1862* . . . (Montgomery, 1862), 18–19, 44; *Acts of the General Assembly of the State of South Carolina, Passed in December, 1862, and February and April, 1863* (Columbia, 1863), 143; *Acts of the General Assembly of the State of Georgia, Passed in . . . November and December, 1861* (Milledgeville, 1862), 66–67; *An Ordinance for Suppressing Oppressive Speculation upon the Present Necessities of the People . . .* (Raleigh, N.C., 1861); *Journal of the Convention of the People of North Carolina, Held on the 20th Day of May, A.D., 1861* (Raleigh, 1862), 75; *Public Laws of the State of North Carolina, Passed by the General Assembly, at Its Session of 1862–'63 . . .* (Raleigh, 1863), 20; *Journal of the Convention of*

the People of Florida, at a Called Session, Begun . . . January 14, 1862 (Tallahassee, 1862), 47–48; The Acts and Resolutions Adopted by the General Assembly of Florida, at Its Eleventh Session, Begun . . . November 18, 1861 (Tallahassee, 1862), 31; General Laws of Ninth Legislature of the State of Texas . . . (Houston, 1862), 56. Brown quoted in Bryan, Confederate Georgia, 41. Georgia also used its tax system to punish extortion. See Peter Wallenstein, From Slave South to New South: Public Policy in Nineteenth-Century Georgia (Chapel Hill, 1987), 113. Some cities also passed their own laws. See "No Speculation in Augusta," Milledgeville (Ga.) Confederate Union, December 1, 1863; "Cheap Provisions," Charleston (S.C.) Mercury, March 21, 1862.

10. An Ordinance for Suppressing Oppressive Speculation, 1; Senate of South Carolina, A Bill to Prohibit Extortion and Punish Extortioners, Preceded by a Report of the Committee on the Judiciary (Columbia, 1863); House of Representatives of South Carolina, Amendment Offered by Mr. Yeadon, to a Bill to Prohibit and Punish Extortioners (Columbia, 1863). Georgia and North Carolina also made specific provision for juries.

11. On the popularity of auctions, see Coulter, Confederate States, 233; and on Virginia's resolution to suppress auctions, see "The Bill Against Auction Sales," Daily Richmond Enquirer, September 17, 1863. For an example of northern labor opposing auctions on similar grounds, see Sean Wilentz, Chants Democratic: New York City & the Rise of the American Working Class, 1788–1850 (New York, 1984), 150–51. Auctions did exist in the Old South, but usually prices and bidding were subject to close community control. The spread of the auction in the Confederacy was accompanied by a dramatic breakdown in these norms.

12. Gregg, A Sermon: Preached in St. David's Church, 3; Religious Herald, December 18, 1862; Minutes of the Synod of South Carolina, 1858–73, November 7, 1862 (MS in Historical Foundation of the Presbyterian Church, Montreat, N.C., hereinafter cited as a Montreat); Minutes of the Thirty-Fourth Convention of the Evangelical Luthern Synod of Virginia . . . (Staunton, 1864), 12. See also Synod of Alabama, 1858–65, October 24, 1863 (MS in Montreat); Hanover Presbytery, 1858–1864, April 11, 1863 (MS in Montreat); Minutes of the Synod of Mississippi 1861–7 (Jackson, 1880), 34. Newspaper quotations from Scrapbook, I, 18; II, 129 (George Bagby Papers, Virginia Historical Society); Children's Friend (April, 1863), 4; Robert Fleming, The Revised Elementary Spelling Book . . . (Atlanta, 1863), 55. See also [Charles Henry Smith], Bill Arp So Called: A Side Show of the Southern Side of the War (New York, 1866), 31–34.

13. Alexander St. Clair Abrams, The Trials of the Soldier's Wife: A Tale of the Second American Revolution (Atlanta, 1864).

14. Ibid., 120, 185, 49.

15. Ibid., 145; John Cochran quoted in William R. Smith, The History and Debates of the Convention of the People of Alabama . . . (Montgomery, 1861), 307.

16. Foote quoted in Coulter, Confederate States, 227; M. J. Michelbacher, A Sermon Delivered on the Day of Prayer . . . (Richmond, 1863), 12–13. For another defense of the Jews, see resolution praising the "kindness and liberality" of the Jews of Charlotte, N.C., in Charleston Daily Courier, June 24, 1861.

17. "Extortioners," Southern Illustrated News, September 26, 1863, p. 100;

Confederate Baptist, October 15, 1862; "The Extortioner," in Memphis *Weekly Avalanche,* January 28, 1862; Mobile *Evening News,* August 29, 1863; Leroy M. Lee, *Our Country—Our Dangers—Our Duty: A Discourse . . . on the National Fast Day . . .* (Richmond, 1863), 22. On Jews in the Confederacy, see Bertram Wallace Korn, *American Jewry and the Civil War* (Philadelphia, 1951); Louis Schmier, "Notes and Documents on the 1862 Expulsion of Jews from Thomasville, Georgia," *American Jewish Archives,* XXXII (April, 1980), 9–22; Richard McMurry, "Rebels, Extortioners and Counterfeiters: A Note on Confederate Judaeophobia," *Atlanta Historical Journal,* XXII (Fall–Winter, 1978), 45–52; Herbert T. Ezekiel, *The Jews of Richmond During the Civil War* (Richmond, 1915).

18. Gregg, *A Sermon: Preached in St. David's Church,* 2. See also Minutes of the Synod of Alabama, October 24, 1862 (MS in Montreat); Danville (Ga.) *Register* quoted in Montgomery *Daily Advertiser,* May 23, 1862. Cobb quoted in *Southern Christian Advocate,* February 11, 1864; Lila Chunn to Willie Chunn, March 20, 1862, in Willie Chunn Papers, Manuscript Department, William R. Perkins Library, Duke University, hereinafter cited as Perkins Library, Duke. See also "Brother Joe and the Ladies," Natchez (Miss.) *Weekly Courier,* November 26, 1862; Elizabeth Fox-Genovese, "Antebellum Southern Households: A New Perspective on a Familiar Question," *Review,* VII (1984), 215–53. A challenge to market values is implicit in the "mania for shoplifting" by women of all classes reported in the Richmond press. See clipping in Scrapbook, V, 131 (George Bagby Papers, Virginia Historical Society). This might be regarded as analogous to the prepolitical "resistance" of slaves stealing from their masters.

19. L. M. Lee, *Our Country—Our Dangers—Our Duty,* 22, 14; Joel W. Tucker, *The Guilt and Punishment of Extortion . . .* (Fayetteville, N.C., 1862), 12; Albert Gallatin Brown, *State of the Country: Speech . . . in the Confederate Senate, December 24, 1863* (Richmond, 1863), 5.

20. *Central Presbyterian,* March 26, 1863; *Biblical Recorder,* June 15, 1864.

21. This debate grew out of C. Vann Woodward's description of the dramatic discontinuities caused by the Civil War, in *Origins of the New South, 1877–1913* (Baton Rouge, 1951), vol. IX in Wendell Holmes Stephenson and E. Merton Coulter (eds.), *A History of the South.* See his assessment of challenges to his thesis, in Woodward, *Thinking Back: The Perils of Writing History* (Baton Rouge, 1986).

22. "Female Highway Robbery," Edgefield (S.C.) *Advertiser,* May 6, 1863. On St. Lucah, see Ebenezer Fain to Hulda Annie Fain Briant, April 14, 1863, in Hulda Annie Fain Briant Papers, Perkins Library, Duke. On riots, see also *Countryman* (Turnwold, Ga.), April 21, 1863; Memphis *Daily Bulletin,* April 28, 1863; *Confederate Baptist,* March 11, 1863; Hahn, *The Roots of Southern Populism,* 128–29; Paul D. Lack, "Law and Disorder in Confederate Atlanta," *Georgia Historical Quarterly,* LX (Summer, 1982), 171–95; Michael Chesson, "Harlots or Heroines? A New Look at the Richmond Bread Riot," *Virginia Magazine of History and Biography,* XCII (April, 1984), 131–75; Emory M. Thomas, *The Confederate State of Richmond: A Biography of the Capital* (Austin, 1971), 119–21; Sallie Brock Putnam, *Richmond During the War: Four Years of Personal Observation* (New York, 1867), 208.

23. E. P. Thompson, "The Moral Economy of the English Crowd in the Eighteenth Century," *Past and Present,* L (February, 1971), 136; *Daily South-*

ern *Guardian*, September 22, 1863; William Lowndes Yancey, *Speeches . . . in the Senate of the Confederate States* (Montgomery, 1862), 52. See also Paul Escott, "The Moral Economy of the Crowd in Confederate North Carolina," *Maryland Historian*, XII (Spring–Summer, 1982), 1–17; James C. Scott, *The Moral Economy of the Peasant: Rebellion and Subsistence in Southeast Asia* (New Haven, 1976); James C. Scott, *Weapons of the Weak: Everyday Forms of Peasant Resistance* (New Haven, 1985); Mallon, *The Defense of Community in Peru's Central Highlands*; Merrill, "Cash Is Good to Eat"; James Henretta, "Families and Farms."

24. Ebenezer Fain to Huldah Annie Fain Briant, April 14, 1863, in Huldah Annie Fain Briant Papers, Perkins Library, Duke; *Countryman* (Turnwold, Ga.), May 3, 1864.

25. *Army and Navy Messenger*, April 1, 1864.

26. *Countryman* (Turnwold, Ga.), April 21, 1863.

27. *Daily Richmond Enquirer*, October 20 and 13, 1863; *Central Presbyterian*, January 29 and 22, 1863.

28. *Daily Richmond Enquirer*, October 13, 1863. See Wilentz, *Chants Democratic*.

29. J. W. Tucker, *The Guilt and Punishment of Extortion . . .* (Fayetteville, N.C., 1862), 5–6.

Chapter 4

1. *Two Sermons on the Times . . . in St. John's Church* (Tallahassee, n.d.), 13–14.

2. Alexander H. Stephens, *A Constitutional View of the Late War Between the States: Its Causes, Character, Conduct and Results* (Philadelphia, 1868); Paul D. Escott, *After Secession: Jefferson Davis and the Failure of Confederate Nationalism* (Baton Rouge, 1978), 35; Michael P. Johnson, *Toward a Patriarchal Republic: The Secession of Georgia* (Baton Rouge, 1977), 33. Stephens first invoked his "corner-stone" image before the war, but he also employed it regularly after secession. See, for example, his address to Atlanta citizens in *Southern Confederacy* (Atlanta, Ga.), March 13, 1861, in which he hails the new Confederate constitution: "We had made African inequality and subordination, and the equality of white men, the chief corner-stone of the Southern republic." Stephens may have been taking this speech on the road, for he spoke at the Atheneum in Savannah eight days later, once again identifying slavery as the "corner-stone" of the new Confederacy, and declaring it to be "the immediate cause of the late rupture and present revolution." Stephens quoted in Charles Robert Lee, Jr., *The Confederate Constitutions* (Chapel Hill, 1963), 110. On European reservations about slavery, see James D. Richardson (ed.), *The Messages and Papers of Jefferson Davis and the Confederacy, Including Diplomatic Correspondence, 1861–1865* (New York, 1966), II, 37, 41, 53, 68. Frank Everson Vandiver, *Their Tattered Flags: The Epic of the Confederacy* (New York, 1970), 24.

3. William R. Smith, *The History and Debates of the Convention of the People of Alabama . . .* (Montgomery, 1861), 229, 196; *Daily Richmond Enquirer*, April 15, 1861; *Journal of the Convention of the State of Arkansas* (Little Rock, Ark., 1861), 44; "A Declaration of the Immediate Causes Which Induce and Justify the Secession of the State of Mississippi from the Federal

Union," in *Journal of the State Convention and Ordinances and Resolutions Adopted in January 1861* . . . (Jackson, 1861), 86; John H. Rice, *A System of Modern Geography*. . . *Expressly for the Use of Schools and Academies in the Confederate States of America* . . . (Atlanta, 1862), 21; Joseph Addison Turner, "The Old Plantation," ed. Henry Prentice Miller, *Emory University Sources and Reprints*, II (1945), 9 (originally published in 1862); "Gamma" [George Bagby], Mobile *Daily Register*, December 31, 1864; *Daily Richmond Enquirer*, November 2, 1864; Augusta *Daily Constitutionalist*, November 17, 1861, quoted in M. P. Johnson, *Toward a Patriarchal Republic*, 127. In a recent study of secession in Virginia and Mississippi, Shearer Davis Bowman concluded that "for all but a small minority of staunchly Unionist slaveowners . . . the 'domestic institution of slavery' was 'of infinitely more vital concern' than questions about 'federal compacts and national unions.'" Bowman, "Slaveholders and the Constitution: Attitudes in Mississippi and Virginia During the Secession Crisis of 1860–61" (Paper presented at the Annual Meeting of the Organization of American Historians, Philadelphia, Pa., April, 1987), kindly lent by the author. For other states' declarations of causes for secession that emphasize slavery, see South Carolina Convention, "Declaration of Causes," *Convention Documents* . . . (Columbia, 1861), 5; *Journal of the Public and Secret Proceedings of the Convention of the People of Georgia* . . . (Milledgeville, 1861), 104–14. Arkansas listed six causes of discontent, all related to slavery in *Journal of Both Sessions of the Convention of the State of Arkansas* . . . (Little Rock, 1861), 52.

4. William A. Hall, *The Historic Significance of the Southern Revolution: A Lecture* . . . (Petersburg, Va., 1864), 14; Stephen Elliott, *Our Cause in Harmony with the Purposes of God in Christ Jesus: A Sermon* . . . (Savannah, 1862), 14; *Address of the Atlanta Daily Register to the People of the Confederate States* (Atlanta, 1864), 4; I. T. Tichenor, *Fast-Day Sermon* . . . *Before the General Assembly of* . . . *Alabama* (Montgomery, 1863), 13; Calvin H. Wiley, *Scriptural Views of National Trials: Or the True Road to the Independence and Peace of the Confederate States of America* (Greensboro, N.C. 1863), 159; *Pastoral Letter from the Bishops of the Protestant Episcopal Church to the Clergy and Laity of the Church in the Confederate States of America* (Augusta, 1862), 10. See also William Holcombe, "The Alternative," *Southern Literary Messenger*, XXXII (February, 1861), 83; William H. Wheelwright, *A Discourse Delivered to the Troops* (Richmond, 1862), 10; George D. Armstrong, *"The Good Hand of Our God upon Us." A Thanksgiving Sermon* . . . (Norfolk, 1861), 10; John Bachman, "Fast–Day Sermon," Charleston *Daily Courier*, June 15, 1861; Elizabeth Fox-Genovese and Eugene D. Genovese, "Religious Ideals of Southern Slave Society," *Georgia Historical Quarterly*, LXX (Spring, 1986), 1–15; and Eugene D. Genovese, *"Slavery Ordained of God": The Southern Slaveholders' View of Biblical History and Modern Politics* (Gettysburg, 1985).

5. Benjamin M. Palmer, *A Discourse Before the General Assembly of South Carolina* . . . (Columbia, 1864), 14; Elliott, *Our Cause in Harmony*, 10; "Proceedings of Secession Convention," *Daily Richmond Enquirer*, December 7, 1861.

6. Charles W. Dabney to Robert L. Dabney, March 16, 1863, Charles W. Dabney Papers, Southern Historical Collection, University of North Carolina, Chapel Hill; T. W. MacMahon, *Cause and Contrast: An Essay on the Ameri-*

can *Crisis* (Richmond, 1862), ix, x. For traditional proslavery themes, see also W. H. Vernor, *A Sermon . . . Before the Marshall Guards . . .* (Lewisburg, Tenn., 1861), 12–13; Alfred A. Watson, *Sermon . . . Before the Annual Council of the Diocese of North Carolina . . .* (Raleigh, 1863); J. J. D. Renfroe, *"The Battle Is God's": A Sermon Preached Before Wilcox's Brigade . . .* (Richmond, 1863); *Address to Christians Throughout the World* (Richmond, 1863); John B. Thrasher, *Slavery a Divine Institution . . .* (Port Gibson, Miss., 1861); *Providential Aspect and Salutary Tendency of the Existing Crisis . . .* (New Orleans, 1861), 12; Augustine Verot, *Slavery and Abolitionism . . .* (St. Augustine, [1861]); John Randolph Tucker, *The Southern Church Justified in Its Support of the South in the Present War . . .* (Richmond, 1863); James Henley Thornwell, *The State of the Country . . .* (Columbia, S.C., 1861); Harrison Berry, *Slavery and Abolitionism, as Viewed by a Georgia Slave . . .* (Atlanta, 1861); Bland [pseud.], *A Southern Document: To the People of Virginia* (Wytheville, 1861).

7. Robert Fleming, *The Revised Elementary Spelling Book . . .* (Atlanta, 1863), 57; *The First Reader, for Southern Schools* (Raleigh, 1864), 16–17; Marinda Branson Moore, *The Geographical Reader, for the Dixie Children* (Raleigh, 1863), 13; R. H. Rivers, *Elements of Moral Philosophy* (Nashville, 1861); *Catalogue of the Officers and Students of Mercer University, 1860–61* (Penfield, Ga., 1861), 31, 32.

8. Clipping from Raleigh *Register*, in Scrapbook, I, 6, (George Bagby Papers, Virginia Historical Society); "A Faithful Servant," Mobile *Evening News*, September 28, 1864; "United Prayer for Our Country," Augusta *Weekly Constitutionalist*, September 11, 1861. See also "A Negro Soldier" and "Incident of the War," in Mary A. Dickinson Scrapbook (Manuscripts Collection, Hill Memorial Library, Louisiana State University, Baton Rouge). H. Berry, *Slavery and Abolitionism*. See also Clarence L. Mohr's excellent analysis of this pamphlet and his revelation of a subversive subtext, in Mohr, *On the Threshold of Freedom: Masters and Slaves in Civil War Georgia* (Athens, Ga., 1986), 58–64. Columbus (Ga.) *Times*, March 23, 1864; Augusta *Daily Constitutionalist*, October 20, 1864. See also Desmos [pseud.], *Old Toney and His Master . . .* (Nashville, 1861).

9. "Philanthropy Rebuked: A True Story," *Southern Confederacy*, clipping in M. J. Solomons Scrapbook, 1861–1863, p. 159 (Manuscript Department, William R. Perkins Library, Duke University); "A Southern Scene from Life," M. J. Solomons Scrapbook, 19.

10. Iline Fife, "The Theatre During the Confederacy" (Ph.D. dissertation, Louisiana State University, 1949), 466, 154, 137, 159; *Daily Richmond Examiner*, September 7, 1864; *Southern Illustrated News*, November 1, 1862, quoted in Richard Barksdale Harwell, *Brief Candle: The Confederate Theatre* (Worcester, Mass., 1971), 45. For a survey of minstrel performers, see Alexander Saxton, "Blackface Minstrelsy and Jacksonian Ideology," *American Quarterly*, XXXVII (January, 1975), 3–28. On minstrelsy in the South, see John Smith Kendall, "New Orleans' Negro Minstrels," *Louisiana Historical Quarterly*, XXX (1947), 128–148, and Harry R. Edwall, "The Golden Era of Minstrelsy in Memphis," *West Tennessee Historical Society Papers*, IX (1955), 29–48.

11. On the history of minstrelsy and its relation to political sentiments on slavery, see Robert C. Toll, *Blacking Up: The Minstrel Show in Nineteenth-*

Century America (New York, 1974). See also Sam Dennison, *Scandalize My Name: Black Imagery in American Popular Music* (New York, 1982), Chaps. II–V.

12. Mobile *Register and Advertiser,* July 25, 1861. For examples and descriptions of Confederate minstrelsy, see the broadsides *One Night More of the Colored Burlesque Minstrels . . . the Confederate Nightingales* (N.p., n.d.), and *Melodeon! . . . The Lone Star Minstrel and Dramatic Troupe!* (Houston, 1861); Chattanooga *Daily Rebel,* July 30, 1863; Mobile *Evening News,* March 28, 1863; Columbus (Ga.) *Times,* March 7, 1864; Natchez (Miss.) *Weekly Courier,* July 30, 1862; Clara Victoria Dargan Maclean Diary, February 15 and November 1, 1861 (Clara Victoria Dargan Maclean Papers, Manuscript Department, William R. Perkins Library, Duke University).

13. Charlie L. Ward, *I'm Coming to My Dixie Home; as Sung by Lincoln's Intelligent Contrabands* (Columbia, S.C., n.d.).

14. John R. Thompson, *The Burial of Latané* (Richmond, 1862); Lucy Ashton to John R. Thompson, August 5, 1862, in John R. Thompson Papers, Virginia Historical Society; "Burial of Latané," *Daily Richmond Enquirer,* October 23, 1864; Richmond *Times Dispatch,* September 19, 1863; Emily Salmon, "The Burial of Latané: Symbol of the Lost Cause," *Virginia Cavalcade,* XXVIII (Winter, 1979), 126.

15. J. R. Thompson, *The Burial of Latané.* On the history painting tradition, see Ann Uhry Abrams, *The Valiant Hero: Benjamin West and Grand-Style History Painting* (Washington, D.C., 1985); Dennis Montagna, "Benjamin West's 'The Death of Wolfe': A Nationalist Narrative," *American Art Journal,* VIII (Spring, 1981), 72–88; Charles Mitchell, "Benjamin West's 'Death of General Wolfe' and the Popular History Piece," *Journal of the Warburg and Courtauld Institutes,* VII (1944) 20–33. I am grateful to Malcolm Campbell for discussing these art-historical issues with me.

16. The slave states provided 93,542 black soldiers to the Union army. See Ira Berlin, Joseph Reidy, and Leslie Rowland (eds.), *Freedom: A Documentary History of Emancipation, 1861–1867. Series II. The Black Military Experience.* (New York, 1982), 12. The "lost" slave is described in Spencer Glasgow Welch, *A Confederate Surgeon's Letters to His Wife* (New York, 1911), 60, 104. See also illusions and denials of James Henry Hammond, discussed in Drew Gilpin Faust, *James Henry Hammond and the Old South: A Design for Mastery* (Baton Rouge, 1982), 369–370, 382. For recent work stressing blacks' liberation efforts during the Civil War, see Armstead Louis Robinson, "Day of Jubilo: Civil War and the Demise of Slavery in the Mississippi Valley, 1861–1865" (Ph.D. dissertation, University of Rochester, 1976); Ira Berlin *et al.* (eds.), *Freedom: A Documentary History of Emancipation, 1861–1867. Series I. Volume 1: The Destruction of Slavery* (New York, 1985); Barbara Jeanne Fields, *Slavery and Freedom on the Middle Ground: Maryland During the Nineteenth Century* (New Haven, 1985); John Cimprich, *Slavery's End in Tennessee, 1861–1865* (University, Ala., 1985); Roberta Sue Alexander, *North Carolina Faces the Freedmen: Race Relations During Presidential Reconstruction, 1865–1867* (Durham, 1985); Leon F. Litwack, *Been in the Storm So Long: The Aftermath of Slavery* (New York, 1979); Eugene D. Genovese, *Roll, Jordan, Roll: The World the Slaves Made* (New York, 1974), 97–112.

17. *Countryman* (Turnwold, Ga.), February 7, 1865; J. J. D. Renfroe, "The Battle Is God's", 17–18; "The Princeton Review on the State of the Country," *Southern Presbyterian Review,* XIV (April, 1861), 9.

18. Joel Berry, quoted in *Proceedings of the Mississippi State Convention* . . . (Jackson, 1861), 87–88; Richmond *Daily Whig*, May 31, 1861. In Georgia, the tax issue was not *ad valorem*, which had been addressed a decade before, but a more generalized increase in the progressive nature of state taxes, with rich Georgians paying a considerably larger proportion of state levies by the end of the war. See Peter Wallenstein, *From Slave South to New South: Public Policy in Nineteenth-Century Georgia* (Chapel Hill, 1987), 110–18. J. Mills Thornton, III, "Fiscal Policy and the Failure of Radical Reconstruction in the Lower South," in J. Morgan Kousser and James M. McPherson (eds.), *Region, Race, and Reconstruction: Essays in Honor of C. Vann Woodward* (New York, 1982), 352–60, offers the best overview of the *ad valorem* movement and its political meaning in the antebellum South. On North Carolina see Marc W. Kruman, *Parties and Politics in North Carolina, 1836–1865* (Baton Rouge, 1983). Taxation initiatives at the national level were limited by the requirement that a census precede apportionment of tax levies. But by 1864, Treasury Secretary Christopher Memminger was arguing for *ad valorem* taxation of land and slaves, even though a census was impossible. This was embodied in the tax bill of February 17, 1864. See Robert Cecil Todd, *Confederate Finance* (Athens, Ga., 1954), 148–50.

19. *Southern Christian Advocate*, May 12, 1864; L. W. Spratt, "Slave Trade in the Southern Congress," *Southern Literary Messenger*, XXXII (June, 1861), 415, 413; *Journal of the Acts and Proceedings of a General Convention of the State of Virginia* (Richmond, 1861), 67; W. R. Smith, *The History . . . of the Convention . . . of Alabama . . .* (Montgomery, 1861), 228–59. See Ronald Takaki, *A Pro-Slavery Crusade: The Agitation to Reopen the African Slave Trade* (New York, 1971).

20. Genovese, *Roll, Jordan, Roll*, 51; Drew Gilpin Faust, *A Sacred Circle: The Dilemma of the Intellectual in the Old South, 1840–1860* (Baltimore, 1977, 1986), 121–22; Bell I. Wiley, "The Movement to Humanize the Institution of Slavery During the Confederacy," *Emory University Quarterly*, V (December, 1949), 207–20; Rosser Taylor, "Humanizing the Slave Code of North Carolina," *North Carolina Historical Review*, II (July 1925), 323–31. See also an excellent discussion of wartime slavery reform in Georgia, in Mohr, *On the Threshold of Freedom*, Chap. 8.

21. Charles Colcock Jones, *Religious Instruction of the Negroes . . .* (Richmond, 1862), 24–25; James A. Lyon, "Slavery and the Duties Growing out of the Relation," *Southern Presbyterian Review*, XVI (July, 1863), 36. See also R. Milton Winter, "James A. Lyon: Southern Presbyterian Apostle of Progress," *Journal of Presbyterian History*, LX (Winter, 1982), 314–35; John K. Bettersworth, "Mississippi Unionism: The Case of the Rev. James A. Lyon," *Journal of Mississippi History*, I (January, 1939), 37–52; James A. Lyon Journal, 1861–1870 (MS in Mitchell Memorial Library, Mississippi State University, Starkville, Miss.); W. Harrison Daniel, "Southern Presbyterians in the Confederacy," *North Carolina Historical Review*, XLIV (July, 1967), 231–55.

22. Zebulon Vance to Calvin Wiley, February 3, 1865, in Calvin H. Wiley Papers, Southern Historical Collection University of North Carolina, Chapel Hill. See also Calvin H. Wiley, *Scriptural Views of National Trials . . .* (Greensboro, N.C., 1863), 189; Minutes of the Roanoke Presbytery, April 18, 1863 (MS in Historical Foundation of the Presbyterian Church, Montreat, N.C.); Henry C. Lay, *Pastoral Letter to the Clergy and Members of the Protestant Episcopal Church in the State of Arkansas* (Memphis, 1861), 14–15;

Minutes of the Seventy-Third Annual Session of the South Carolina Confer-
ence of the Methodist Episcopal Church . . . (Charleston, 1861), 25–26; *Re-*
ligious Herald, May 7, 1863; Lyon, "Slavery and the Duties Growing Out of
the Relation," 14; Wiley, *Scriptural Views,* 197.
        23. *Minutes of the Forty-fifth Session of the Alabama Baptist Association*
. . . *1864* (Montgomery, 1864), 7; *Biblical Recorder,* September 24, 1862; Marinda Branson Moore, *The Dixie Speller* . . . (Raleigh, 1864), 37, and *The Geo-*
graphical Reader . . . , 14. For contemporary acknowledgments of war-born
changes in the proslavery argument, see Wiley, *Scriptural Views,* 193, and
James O. Andrew, "Thoughts for the Fast Day," *Southern Christian Advocate,*
March 26, 1863.
        24. George Foster Pierce and B. M. Palmer, *Sermons* . . . *Delivered Before*
the General Assembly . . . (Milledgeville, Ga. 1863), 14–15; Tichenor, *Fast-*
Day Sermon, 11; A. W. Miller, "Report on the State of the Church: A Paper
Read Before the Synod of Virginia . . . 1862," *Southern Presbyterian Review,*
XV (January, 1863), 447. See also Samuel K. Talmage, "Should the Law Be
Repealed Prohibiting Teaching Our Slaves to Read the Bible," Milledgeville
Confederate Union, October 28, 1862.
        25. "Educated Negroes," *Countryman* (Turnwold, Ga.), November 17,
1862; "A Slave Marriage Law," *Southern Presbyterian Review,* XVI (October,
1863), 147.
        26. Mohr, *On the Threshold of Freedom,* 262; Robinson, "Day of Jubilo,"
548; David Brion Davis, *Slavery and Human Progress* (New York, 1984), 8. For
examples of the inefficiencies and inconsistencies of prewar slave management, see Drew Gilpin Faust, *James Henry Hammond,* Part II. For examples of
differing definitions of slavery in different cultural and historical contexts, see
Orlando Patterson, *Slavery and Social Death: A Comparative Study* (Cambridge, 1982), and Susanne Miers and Igor Kopytoff (eds.), *Slavery in Africa:*
Historical and Anthropological Perspectives (Madison, 1977).
        27. Eric Foner, *Nothing but Freedom: Emancipation and Its Legacy* (Baton
Rouge, 1983); Hughes, quoted in Bertram Wyatt-Brown, "Modernizing Southern Slavery: The Proslavery Argument Reinterpreted," in J. Morgan Kousser
and James M. McPherson (eds.), *Region, Race and Reconstruction: Essays in*
Honor of C. Vann Woodward (New York, 1982), 37.
        28. Pierce and Palmer, *Sermons,* 14–15.

Index

Abolitionism, 30, 58, 60, 62, 69, 79
Abrams, Alexander St. Clair, 48–49
Africanisms, 11
Age, 7
Alabama: state convention in, 35, 36, 37, 39; citizenship restrictions, 36; conservatism of, 37; legislation to control extortion, 46; slave-trade issue, 74
American War of Independence, 14
Anderson, Benedict, 16, 18
Arkansas, 35, 37
Atkinson, Thomas, 42
Atlanta *Daily Register*, 7
Auctions, 47
Augusta *Daily Constitutionalist*, 60
Augusta *Weekly Constitutionalist*, 63
Augustine, 23–24

Bagby, George, 38, 47, 60
Beauregard, P. G. T., 18
Bercovitch, Sacvan, 27
Berry, Harrison, 63
Bible, 28–29
Biblical Recorder, 24
Bilbo, William, 7, 15
Britain. *See* Great Britain
Brown, Joseph, 35, 46, 78
Burial of Latané, 69–71

Calhoun, John C., 36
Caribbean Islands, 80
Central Presbyterian, 45, 46, 55, 57
Channing, Steven, 2, 4
Charleston *Mercury*, 11, 74
Children's Friend, 48
Christian Observer, 24
Christianity: clergy's authority, 22–23, 28, 81; just war tradition, 23–24, 26; fast days, 26–29; biblical analogies for Confederate nationalism, 28–29; antebellum South, 29–30; view of war as retribution for sins, 30–31; clergy's antidemocratic rhetoric, 32–33; and reform, 41; views of extortion, 42, 44–45, 51–52, 55–57; and slavery, 60–62, 75–77, 81;

and Confederate nationalism, 82–83. *See also* Clergy; Evangelicalism
Churches. *See* Christianity
Civil War: music and, 18–19; just war tradition, 23–24, 26, 60; as crusade, 28; as divine retribution, 30–31, 41; and commercial expansion in the South, 44; riots during, 52, 54–55, 56; southern explanations of, 59
Clark, William, 78
Clemens, Samuel. *See* Twain, Mark
Clergy: authority of, 22–23, 28, 81; antidemocratic rhetoric of, 32–33; views on sin of extortion, 42, 44–45, 51–52, 56–57; view on love of money, 58; views on slavery, 60–62, 72–73, 75–77, 81. *See also* Christianity
Cobb, Howell, 51
Columbus, Georgia, *Times*, 63
Confederacy: reasons for defeat of, 1–2, 3–4; belief system of, 2, 5; popular interests and, 15–16, 21, 35, 83; as divinely chosen, 26–29; identification with American nationalism, 26–27; biblical analogies for, 28–29; antidemocratic tendencies of, 32–40; class differences, 34–35, 39, 51–52, 82; state conventions and, 34; citizenship restrictions, 36–37; sins of, 41–42, 58; and sin of greed, 44–57; legislation to control extortion, 45–46; contradictions in, 57; slave-trade issue, 74–75
Confederate nationalism: debate over, 2–4, 5, 6; spurious nature of, 3–4; approach for the study of, 6–7; creation of, 7–8, 10, 14–15, 21, 39, 84–85; role of newspapers in, 7–8; European influences on, 10; racial determination of, 10–11; language reform and, 11; parallels with other independence movements, 11, 13–14; class interests and, 15–16, 21, 34–35, 82; communication

difficulties and, 16–18, 21; problem of, 19, 21; purposes served by, 21; Christianity and, 22–23, 39, 82–83; as divine mandate, 27–28, 60–61, 82–83; biblical analogies for, 28–29; covenant theology and, 28–29, 82; contradictions in, 39–40, 57, 82–84; reform as central to, 41; slavery's importance to, 58–62, 81; power and change, 82–85
Coulter, E. Merton, 1, 17
Countryman, 72, 78

Daily Richmond Enquirer, 13, 18, 33, 55, 56, 60
Daily Richmond Examiner, 50, 65
Danville Register, 51
Davis, David Brion, 80
Davis, Jefferson: inauguration of, 8, 14; and postal issues, 17; music written about, 19; calls for God's aid, 24, 33; defense of Civil War, 24; and extortion, 46; de-emphasis on importance of slavery, 59
DeBow's Review, 10, 17
Degler, Carl, 3

Elliott, Stephen, 23–24, 27, 30, 60, 61
England. See Great Britain
English language. See Language
Escott, Paul, 59
Evangelicalism, 22, 23, 32, 57, 82, 83, 84
Extortion: sinful nature of, 41–43; in the North, 42–43; clergy's view of, 44–45, 47, 51–52, 56–57; during the Civil War, 44–45; legislation to control, 45–47, 55–56; poetry about, 47–48; novel about, 48–49, 51; Jews and, 50, 51; differences between men and women, 51; riots and, 52, 54–55

Fascists, 5
Fast days, 26–29
Feminism, 30

Fichte, Johann, 10
Fiction. See Novels
Fleming, Robert, 62
Florida, 37, 46
Foner, Eric, 80
Foote, Henry, 50
France, 6, 11, 13, 61
French Revolution, 6, 11, 13

Geertz, Clifford, 5
Genovese, Eugene, 3, 75
Georgia: state convention in, 35; constitutional convention in, 37; commercial expansion in, 43; legislation to control extortion, 46; slavery reform legislation, 78; slavery in, 79, 81
Goode, T. F., 59
Great Britain, 13, 61
Greece, 13
Greed. See Extortion
Gregg, Alexander, 45, 47, 52

Harvie, Lewis, 61
Herder, Johann von, 10
Hughes, Henry, 80

Ideology, 4–5. See also Confederate nationalism
Italy, 5, 13, 15

Jamison, David Flavel, 10
Jews, 45, 50, 51
Johnson, Michael, 37, 59
Jones, Charles Colcock, Jr., 31, 75–76
Jones, J., 28
Journalism. See Newspapers; names of specific newspapers
Just war tradition, 23–24, 26, 60

Lamartine, Alphonse de, 10
Language, 11
Lee, Mrs. Robert E., 8
Leutze, Emanuel, 70
Lincoln, Abraham, 44, 69
Literacy, 17, 18, 21, 78
Lost Cause, Myth of, 2
Lynchburg Virginian, 47

MacMahon, T. W., 62
Materialism. *See* Extortion
Mexico, 13
Michelbacher, Maximilian, 50
Michelet, Jules, 10
Miller, Perry, 27
Ministers. *See* Clergy
Minstrelsy, 65, 67, 69
Mississippi, 46, 73, 78
Mobile *Evening News*, 30, 63
Mobile *Register*, 60
Mobile *Register and Advertiser*, 67
Mohr, Clarence, 79
Montgomery *Daily Advertiser*, 8,
  29, 45
Montgomery *Daily Mail*, 8
Moore, Marinda, 62
Music, 18–19, 65, 67, 69
Myth of the Lost Cause, 2

Napoleon, 13
Nationalism: anthropological study
  of, 4–5; creation of culture and,
  5–6; symbols of, 5–6; nineteenth-century movement, 10,
  13; requirements for, 16, 84; and
  just war tradition, 23. *See also*
  Confederate nationalism
Nazis, 5
Netherlands, 13
New Orleans *Crescent*, 38
New South Creed, 2
Newspapers: role of, 7–8; difficulties in publication of, 17–18; free
  mailing to soldiers, 17; accounts
  of slavery in, 63. *See also* names
  of specific newspapers
North: portrayal as Saxons, 10–11;
  reform movements, 30; sinful nature of, 30–31, 35, 39; materialism of, 42, 43, 50, 58
North Carolina: state convention
  in, 35, 36, 37; citizenship restrictions, 36; conservatism of, 37;
  legislation to control extortion,
  46; taxation of slaves, 73
Novels, 48–49, 51

Painting, 69–71
Palmer, Benjamin, 61

Pierce, George Foster, 31, 77, 81
Pinckney, Charles Cotesworth, 42
Poetry, 47–48, 63–65, 69–70
Poland, 13
Potter, David, 2–3
Press. *See* Newspapers
Printing industry, 17–18, 21
Publishing industry, 17–18, 21
Puritans, 26–27, 29, 43

Raleigh *Register*, 63
Religion. *See* Christianity
Religious Herald, 30, 47
Renfroe, J. J. D., 72
Republicanism, 30–32, 82, 83, 84
Revolutionary War. *See* American
  War of Independence
Richmond *Age*, 7
Richmond *Daily Dispatch*, 38
Richmond *Whig*, 38, 74
Riots, 52, 54–55, 56
Robinson, Armstead, 79
Ruffin, Thomas, 37

Scott, Sir Walter, 10, 11
Secession conventions, 34–38, 59–
  60
Sellers, Charles, 3
Sicily, 13
Simms, William Gilmore, 14
Slave trade, 74–75
Slaveowners, 15–16, 34, 35, 39, 52,
  74
Slavery: punishment for, 2; South's
  beliefs regarding, 4, 5; slaves' language, 11; and class issues, 34;
  treatment in popular works, 49;
  63–71; views on extortion and,
  57; importance of, 58–60; de-
  emphasis on importance of, 59;
  divine sanction of, 60–62;
  educational treatment of, 62–63,
  77; newspaper accounts of, 63; in
  poetry, 63–65; in popular music,
  65; slave insurrections, 67; in
  painting, 69–71; discrepancy between ideology and reality, 71;
  portrayal of slaves' loyalty, 71–
  72; benefits for nonslaveholders,
  72–73; clergy's views on, 72–73,

75–76; taxation of, 73–74; re-
form measures, 75–81; opposi-
tion to reform legislation, 78–79;
paternalistic ethos of, 82
*Smith and Barrow's Monthly Mag-
azine*, 7–8
Socialism, 30
Songs. *See* Music
South. *See* Confederacy
South Carolina, 35–36, 43, 46
Southern Christian Advocate, 22
Southern Illustrated News, 50
Southern Literary Messenger, 7, 16,
47, 70
Southern Monthly, 17
Southern nationalism. *See* Con-
federate nationalism
Southern Presbyterian Review, 13,
73, 78
Spain, 13
Speech. *See* Language
Spratt, L. W., 74–75
Stampp, Kenneth, 3
State constitutions, 34–38
State conventions, 34–38, 59–60
Stephens, Alexander, 59

Taxation, 73–74
Texas, 46
Thomas, Emory, 5
Thompson, E. P., 52, 54
Thompson, John R., 69–70
Thornwell, James Henley, 31, 41
Tichenor, I. T., 77

Toombs, Robert, 13
Trials of the Soldier's Wife
(Abrams), 48–49, 51
Tucker, Henry, 30
Tucker, J. W., 56
Turner, Joseph Addison, 55, 72, 78
Turner, Nat, 67
Twain, Mark, 10

Vance, Zebulon, 76, 78
Vandiver, Frank, 59
Vietnam War, 3
Virginia: state convention in, 35,
36, 37–39; citizenship restrictions, 36; suffrage in, 37–38; conservatism of, 39; legislation to
control extortion, 46, 55, 56; taxation of slaves, 73; slave-trade issue, 74

Warranteeism, 80
Wars. *See* American War of Inde-
pendence; Civil War; Vietnam
War
Washington, George, 14, 24
Washington, William D., 69–70
West, Benjamin, 70
West Virginia, 38
Wiley, Calvin, 31, 76
Winthrop, John, 27
Women, 51, 52, 54–55

Yancey, William Lowndes, 54
Yelverton, G. T., 59